Automatic

"Automatic" Y'all

Weaver D's Guide to the Soul

DEXTER WEAVER

with

Patrick Allen

Hill Street Press

Athens, Georgia

To Foxy Roxy

Weaver D

A HILL STREET PRESS BOOK

Hill Street Press LLC
191 East Broad Street, Suite 209
Athens, Georgia 30601-2848 USA
706-613-7200   www.hillstreetpress.com

Hill Street Press is committed to preserving the written word. Every effort is
made to print on acid-free paper with a significant amount of recycled content.

Text and cover design by Anne Richmond Boston.

Printed in the United States of America.

Library of Congress Cataloging-in-Publication Data

Weaver, Dexter (Dexter McKindley), 1954–

    Automatic y'all : Weaver D's guide to the soul / by Dexter Weaver ;
in conversation with Patrick Allen .
            p.   cm.
    ISBN 1-892514-27-3 (alk. paper)
    1. Afro-American cookery. 2. Weaver, Dexter (Dexter McKindley),
1954– . I. Allen, Patrick (James Patrick), 1965– . II. Title.
TX715.W354 1999
641.59'296073—dc21   99-36685
                                       CIP

ISBN # 1-892514-27-3

10 9 8 7 6 5 4 3 2 1

First edition

Contents

Acknowledgments

I want to say "hey!" to all the following for their kind help in making this book come together: Patrick Allen, Walter Allen Jr., Anne Richmond Boston, Nathan Bowden, Sweetie Clark, Mildred Dillard, Caitlin Gal, Rita Hector, Paige Otwell, Jennifer Patrick, Randy Pattman, Adam Paul of the Baltimore Transit Archives, Tom Payton, Bob Sweeney, Jason Thrasher, Nelson Wells and the crew at Team Clermont, and Gabriel T. Wilmoth.

I want to thank my mother, Carrie Jackson, for leading me as a child, standing behind me as a youngster, and walking beside me as an adult.

The author and the publisher gratefully acknowledge the following for permission to reprint song lyrics appearing the the book:

"We're Gonna Make It": by Billy Davis, Carl Smith, Raynard Miner, and Gene Barge; courtesy of Chevis-Shada Publishing Corp., BMI

"Dancing in the Streets": by Marvin Gaye, George Ivy Hunter, and William Stevenson; courtsey of EMI April Music, Inc., BMI

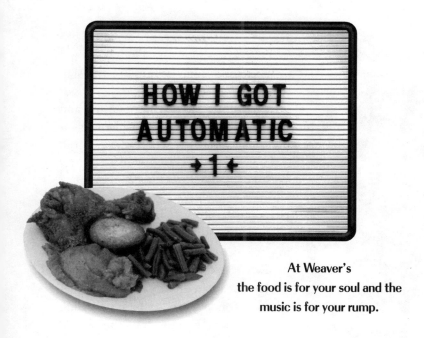

HOW I GOT AUTOMATIC
✦1✦

**At Weaver's
the food is for your soul and the
music is for your rump.**

✦SOMETIMES at the end of the workday, I'll sit my tired self down and ask myself, "I swear I was in three places all day, but how did I get here?" I spend all twenty-five hours in a day cooking up the best good food at my restaurant, grinning and skinning at catering jobs, and managing that employee cafeteria we all call The Happy Kitchen. It seems like a daily miracle but somehow I work it out. Automatic. But tonight is one night Weaver can't even give a good guess as to how I got here.

There's Miss Whitney Houston over there being cute with Patti LaBelle. There's Ike Turner, Dorothy Norwood, and Peabo Bryson. And there's that Boy George, Les Brown, Al B. Sure, and Teddy Pendergrass. I got Snoop Doggy Dog in front of me and Pop Staple of The Staple Singers at my back. Weaver D is at the Grammys! Sitting here with my younger sister Tamara with her little diva self wearing a purple fox fur cape she bought at the same boutique where Rick James buys his furs. The music and the lights. It's a long haul from Athens, Georgia, I tell you what.

Starting about eight years ago, some-wheres around 1986, some nice young people started coming into the restaurant I'd just opened back in my home-town of Athens. At first I didn't seem to notice them any kind of way. They started being frequent and it looks like one of 'em had a convertible. I'm trying to think was it a Corvair or something, let me just say a convertible. They called themselves R.E.M. Definitely a convertible, that much I remember. And they would come down to the restau-

"I'm so excited!" Going to do the Grammy's, dressed like I was ready to meet the King of Kings. I'm in the lobby of the Milford Plaza Hotel in New York City in 1994.

rant for my home-style food and looks like to me they were just a band that was somewhat starting out, getting started, just like I was at the time. They had a record contract and some albums out, but they still weren't truly established. I had my name on my own sign over my own restaurant, but I was struggling then too.

Back in those lean early days I could only afford to buy enough produce and meat to get me through one day's rush at a time. My mother, Carrie Jackson, who has always helped me at the restaurant, would empty the cash register at the end of the night and, tired as we were, off she and I'd go to the Piggly Wiggly store to buy the ingredients we needed to get us through the next day. Only enough and no more. (We just had to hope the day after tomorrow would take care of itself and when payroll came due there'd be enough for that too.) I've always had an open-plan kitchen and customers could see straight-shot from the cash register to the kitchen where I had a glass-front refrigerator. I didn't want my customers to look into some ole Mother Hubbard refrigerator, bare and empty. That just doesn't look good and welcoming like a kitchen should. You don't want to go to a party where there is one dried-up old cheeseball sitting over there in the corner and a couple of raggedy potato chips forlorn in a bowl. I wanted Weaver D's to be a place where there is a bounty, a land flowing with milk and honey, like Moses talked about in Exodus. So back then when we opened a tin can we always opened it from the bottom, emptied it, washed it out real good, and stacked it right up in the front of the refrigerator. Now that looked like a bountiful harvest.

So R.E.M. and their staff started to frequenting the place, and some kind of way they wanted to exchange T-shirts with us during Christmas. We swapped out Weaver D's T-shirts for R.E.M. T-shirts, some kind of a swap like that, either that or food for shirts. Now I'll admit to you from the get-go I really didn't know who they were so maybe I was thinking they were getting the good end of the bargain. I have to say they were a little scruffy looking. Their singer could have run a comb through his hair once or twice. But they were all frequenting the place and they and all the people they brought over were all very nice young people. But mostly vegetarians, not eating meat, not even pork. Bill Berry and Michael Stipe, they're vegetarians. Weaver does not play that. Vegetarians are all the time claiming they're getting all the protein from the beans, but there's no substitute. What's the first thing I think when I see some of these vegetarians? "Bring your skinny, ashy selves to Weaver D's and get some of the real thing." But I always am very honest with the people when they say, "Is any of this cooked with pork or with any kind of meat drippings?" I say, "Oh yeah." They'll most likely ask, "Well what things are not cooked with pork or drippings?" And I always say, "Potato salad, rice, buttered potatoes, squash casserole, sweet potatoes." Now that's a good meal right there. Most vegetarians, they'll come in and get those items, but some of those vegetarians'll eat a little pork if the pig has his back turned. Lot of 'em will say, "I know they got drippings in 'em, but I gotta have some of them collards." So looks like they do a little slipping and sliding just a little bit.

Now if you frequent Weaver D's Delicious Fine Foods you'll know I'm automatic. Everything about me is automatic. When you walk through the front door, you know you'll get some good food like you're supposed to, food that's automatic for the people. After every one of my customers places an order, I get the money in hand and say, "Thank you. Automatic." And I mean every word. You hire Weaver D's to cater your wedding, your CD release party, your fraternity homecoming, and you know Weaver will be there in white top and black bottom with the good food, automatic. If you need a smile or have a problem that we can work out, that's automatic too.

Now some kind of way, that appealed to R.E.M. I suppose because they've always been automatic too. Whenever they put out an album it goes to the top of the charts, automatic. And they have been so good for Athens, supporting the community and the charities, for the people. Also I've seen those R.E.M. boys all over town with their mamas and daddies and grandmamas. They all seem so good to their families, automatic for their people.

So I guess that my slogan appealed to them and they asked me one time could they use my little "Automatic for the

People" saying for one of their albums. "Well, sure you can. Being automatic for the people has brought me nothing but success, happiness, and good feelings, and I hope it does the same for you." So that album was released and, you know it did, it went to the top of the charts *automatic*. It was so good for our hometown boys. R.E.M. toured the world and the world toured me. All the folks from Germany, England, Norway, Sweden, Australia and every which where wanted to come to Athens to see all the R.E.M. sites like the 40 Watt Club where they played their first gig and the first stop on those sightseers' trips *had* to be Weaver D's. They came piled up in campers and tour buses, with video cameras and little kids.

My half-sister, Tamara Weaver, in her purple fox fur diva stole. She bought it at the same store in New York City where Rick James and Diana Ross buy their furs.

Well, I guess you can guess the rest of that story. The album got bigger and bigger and got nominated for a Grammy Award for the Best Album of the Year for 1994. A Grammy, that's the biggest award in music there is practically. And R.E.M. made sure that Weaver got invited to the big ceremony at Radio City

Music Hall in New York City. That is Southern manners for you. Polite and spreading the thank you's around.

Now all that is how R.E.M. came to be knowing me and how they got automatic. But what I want to tell you is how Weaver D got automatic his *own* self. There is a lot of hard work involved and what I haven't been able to do for myself or my family couldn't help with, the Lord has provided.

When little Weaver was shining shoes for thirty-five cents on the street corner in Baltimore, if someone had told me that one day I would be sitting at the Grammy Awards at Radio City Music Hall in New York City, a guest of one of the top bands in the whole worldwide, with my own restaurant waiting on me back home, would I have been surprised? This little Weaver, going to Wardleave Junior High School on the north side of Baltimore, eating those government cheese sandwiches? No, no it wouldn't have surprised me at all. Maybe the particulars, maybe the details. But this little Weaver has always been on his way and as long as I walked in a straight line I knew I was going forward.

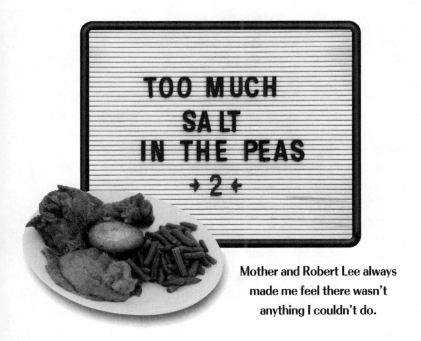

TOO MUCH SALT IN THE PEAS

✦ 2 ✦

Mother and Robert Lee always made me feel there wasn't anything I couldn't do.

→SOMETIMES you can look at children playing "Schoolhouse" and tell in five minutes flat what they'll be when they grow up. Of course the one who's gravitated to the head of the class telling the other little students "go this way" and "go that way" like my half-sister Sharon always did, yes, she'll more than likely grow up to be a teacher in real life, just like Sharon. The boy who is squirming in his seat, running over everyone to answer the question, wheeling and dealing to get out of punishment, maybe he'll be some kind of politician. That serious little child who likes to talk and convince everyone, he's got the spark of a preacher.

One of the first things I really loved to play at was making a full-course meal. At three, I was busy making secret-recipe mudpies (with "greens" made from dried grass clippings) in our front yard in Athens. Just take a handful of dirt or that heavy red clay we have in Georgia, mix it up with some water in an old margarine container or a cracked mixing bowl from your mother's kitchen. Pat it into the shape of a teacake and let it dry out on the hot sidewalk. I guess if I'd thought about it I would have played at selling them too.

Later, my Grandmama Rena Bradley would say, "You would go out there with short pants on and those big pretty Weaver legs of yours. You'd have on the white bucks that your mother done bought you at Lamar Lewis Shoe Store downtown—you don't have no arch in your feet and your mother bought you *good* shoes—and you would go out of that house just clean and shining white and you'd come right back in the house the same way you went out. No dirt be on your hands and none on those white buck shoes."

She also said that I threw rocks at everyone who came down Reese Street. I was getting real good at rock-throwing until I hit my own Grandmama Rena in the head.

Grandmama felt her head and I had drawn her blood. When I saw my grandmama was coming at me, I ran in the house and got in the bed with Great-grandmama Emily Bradley.

My great-grandmama was in the bed sick with cancer of the breast and I knew I'd be safe from a whopping in there with her.

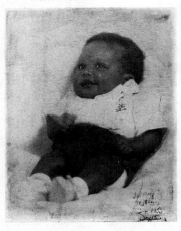

So sweet at four months old.
Ain't that something?

My Grandmama Rena came in and said, "Now let him go, mama, that child has drawn my blood."

Great-grandmama said, "Now don't you be hitting my baby Dexter, Rena."

I won the battle, but not the war. I had to get out of Great-grandmama Emily's sickbed sometime and when I did, you know Grandmama Rena broke me of that rock-throwing real quick. For real.

That's where I spent my growing up years, in Athens, in Clarke County, Georgia, about sixty miles northeast of Atlanta. I was born there in 1954 to Carrie Emily Bradley and Hershel McKindley "Bo" Weaver. I'm the big brother to three surviving half-sisters: Sharon, Tamara, and Janice; and to a half-sister Wanda, who passed in 1992. My half-brother is named Terry. My mother and father split up when I was pretty young but I spent all my growing-up summers with my father and his people.

When I was five years old or so and Great-grandmama Emily was off and on sick in the bed with her cancer, my mother went to Norfolk, Virginia, to work. I was at home with her mama, my Grandmama Rena, and my maternal great-grandmother, Great-grandmama Emily. Great-grandmama Emily was watching me from in the bed while Grandmama Rena was out working and making a living. One day I was hungry and Great-grandmama got hungry too. From her bed she told me how to cook up some English peas. This was one of her favorite things and something she still had a taste for, sick as she was. I was the little cook even back then and I thought I could improve on Great-grandmama's instructions. We had a nice heavy box of salt next to the stove and with me being so young I didn't know when to stop. I really worked those peas with that salt. But we were hungry and both doing the

Me in my little bow tie.
Merry Christmas, Grandmama!

best we could. Her giving instructions from the bed and little Weaver trying to cook for his great-grandmama the best he could. Yes, those English peas were just as salty as they could be. Enough to bring a tear to your eye. Great-grandmama Emily passed in 1959 and I miss her to this day.

My paternal grandfather, Granddaddy Hamp, was the one who taught me to clean rabbits when I was ten years old. He taught me how to run to where the rabbit is in the hutch, they're fast little things, and catch 'em and bring 'em out.

Now if you're squeamish you not might want to read this next part. You make a cut through the fur right under the neck. You just grab them by the neck and start taking the skin off from the neck and work your way down. It's easy.

My aunts, they try and be cute about skinning rabbits, but they have *done* it. As soon as they got out of not *havin'* to do it to please their daddies, they stopped. But down in Washington, Georgia, they all have done it. When, you know, your dad says you are gonna clean these rabbits, you aren't gonna argue with him. Back then you wouldn't, not if you wanted to be able to sit down the next week, you know what I mean.

My grandmama on my dad's side, Grandmama Francis, was big into canning. After mother and I moved to Baltimore, I always went back to Athens on school vacations and I remember that all summer long she put up everything in sight, tomatoes, peaches, pole beans, blackberries, bread and butter pickles, just everything. If she's doing her canning for the season, you don't want to stand still too long in Grandmama Francis's kitchen less you be put up in a Mason jar too. She never taught me how to can, but I know how to pick and peel those peaches. We would go down there to the peach orchard out in Bishop, Georgia, and pick big ole tubs of peaches and bring 'em home and Grandmama would put up a lot of 'em, make peach jellies, jams, and preserves, and even pickled peaches. In the middle of the winter Grandmama could have peaches as fresh as in summertime. What she didn't put up for the cold weather, she would make into a peach cobbler. She'd roll that crust out and put the sugar and the cinnamon on the top and the butter. *Yum!*

A few of my older aunts know how to can but those younger ones say, "I'll learn how to can when Miss Libby and Mr. Del Monte hang up their 'Closed for Business' signs." I always say, "Y'all better be learnin'," but they aren't interested. Which is a shame, because I can taste Grandmama Francis's peach preserves just thinking about it.

Those are some of the kitchen skills I learned when I was down in Athens during those school vacations, skills that people are getting away from now.

Mother met Robert Lee Eberhart early in 1960. And right from the beginning Robert Lee took me as his son. My own father was not so much around then so Robert Lee was a blessing for a boy. He was a big, tall man, not a mean man, but strong-like. So if Robert Lee was on your side, that's all you needed in the neighborhood. Mother always took good care of me by herself but I felt a little bit more protected by Robert Lee. Protected, even if he couldn't always provide. Robert Lee loved to listen to Little Milton and all his old songs: "A Possum in My Tree," "You Left a Goldmine for a

Golddigger," "The Cradle Is Robbin' Me," "Like a Rooster on a Hen," "Grits Ain't Groceries," all those good songs. Robert Lee always sang one Little Milton song, we had the Checker label 45 from '65, called "We're Gonna Make It" that sort of became our family song.

> We might not have a cent to pay the rent,
> but we gonna make it.
> I know we will.
> We may have to eat beans every day,
> but we gonna make it.
> I know we will.

> And if a job is hard to find
> and we have to stand in the welfare line,
> I got your love and you know you got mine.
> So we're gonna make it.
> I know we will.

> We may not have a home to call our own,
> but we gonna make it.
> I know we will.
> We may have to fight hardships galore,
> but we gonna make it.
> I know we will.

But togetherness brings peace of mind—
We can't stay down all the time.
I got your love and you know you got mine,
So we're gonna make it.
I know we will.

Our car may be old, our two rooms cold,
but we gonna make it.
I know we will.
We may not can spare a roach a crumb,
but we gonna make it.
I know we will.

And if I have to carry round a sign
Saying "Help the deaf, the dumb, and the
    blind"
I got your love and you know you got mine,
So we're gonna make it.
I know we will.

Singing that song was Robert Lee's way, you know, of saying no matter what, whether we have heating oil in the tank, food on the table, we were gonna survive. Robert Lee suffered from multiple sclerosis back when not too much was known about it and there wasn't a real treatment to speak of. This kept him from regular work and he got disability checks and such from the government, but they didn't go too far. We got down so low a lot of times that we had to resort to that box of government cheese and that SPAM that Robert Lee used to get.

You know that when you had to take a government cheese and SPAM sandwich to school, you had better hide it from the rest of the children 'cause they would really talk about that SPAM. And then also President Nixon used to have that beef in a can to give out. When Robert Lee got that, some kind of way Mother really knew how to spice that up and put a little barbecue sauce on it and serve it over rice with salt and pepper and a little chopped onion and make a good meal.

Still, every time I hear that Little Milton song, *mmm*, it just turns my mind back to Robert Lee. Due to the MS, Robert Lee passed back in 1989 when he was still pretty young, at age fifty-seven. Sometimes down at the restaurant early on Saturday mornings before we open up, I'll be breading the fried chicken or chopping up onions and listening to WALR 104.7 from Atlanta and they'll be playing that song by Little Milton. I'll say, "Mama, listen to that song." And then Little Milton will get to that line, "We might have to eat beans every day, but we gonna make it." And it's just . . . My eyes might be tearing up a little from those onions.

In 1960, Mother and I moved into the Rocksprings Homes, a government housing project in Athens. We were some of the first residents to live there and it was a real nice place for a single mother trying to raise a son. Clean and tidy, and the people who needed that housing kept it nice. Today the same complex is just torn up and you wouldn't drive through it at sixty miles per hour without counting your hubcaps afterward. It's hard to believe it's the same place. Mother and Robert Lee got on real well together and he and I did too, so he started staying with us at Rocksprings.

When mother first met Robert Lee his multiple sclerosis made him walk with a limp, but when I was a little kid he could still get around real well and he could drive a car.

He took time with me and fetched me to school and brought me home a lot, and ran me wherever else I needed to go. I had put a marble in my ear when I was just a few years old, you know how kids are, and it gave me hearing loss. I had to go through some kind of treatment to make sure I'd be all right with that. Robert Lee took me to the doctor whenever I needed to go. Just like a father would.

Sometimes I would walk in on Robert Lee talking to his sister Fanny Maud Mosby and he'd be telling her all this stuff like "Dexter did this" and "Dexter did that." Like Mother, he always made me feel that there wasn't nothing I couldn't do. Just from him telling me that as a little one, I still believe it today. I remember one year I told him I wanted an electric organ, a little Hammond organ with all the notes marked on the keys, A, B, C, D, and all like that.

He got me one. And that Christmas Day, Fanny Maud and them walked in our house and just stared at me, pumping out songs on that little electric Hammond organ.

And that Robert Lee could really cook some food. Robert Lee did things like pig ears, pig feet, anything with pig. He'd cook a roast so juicy, he called it his "Tender as a Mother's Love Roast." Even after we moved to Baltimore, we still had a lot of the South in us, and for Sunday we was always having some fresh collard or turnip greens, fried chicken, corn pudding, you know, all that good food.

We were living on Collington Avenue in Baltimore and when I came home from school one day I found turtles climbing all over our white marble stoop and our screen door, one of those wrought-iron screen doors like they had in those row houses in Baltimore. I'm not saying they *came* to our house, the turtles. Robert Lee went somewhere and got 'em, intending that good meat for turtle soup. Turtle can taste like chicken, fish, pork, or beef, depending on how you season it. Robert Lee would also do up some rabbits, some squirrels, do up whatever kind of game he could get in the North. Anything the South had to offer that a body could get up North, Robert Lee and Fanny Maud and the Baltimore branch of the Eberharts all knew where to get it. If you wanted hare meat they knew how to get you a good fresh rabbit, even in the North. To this day, I still don't know how.

TEACHER'S PET

+ 3 +

In the ghetto, your notebook is
your treasure chest.

+I STARTED grade school in 1962 at West Broad Street Elementary School in Athens. My mother walked me hand in hand to school. I remember that first day in Miss Harley's class perfectly.

Probably the best part of the school day for me was that mid-day treat. Mother would give me money every day to get a half-pint carton of milk and one of those little Lance-brand Moon Pies. They came in chocolate and vanilla and it would be hard for me to decide which is better.

Don't forget this was back when it was sort of tough in the South for poor folks, I mean hard making money and

Look at me with my Christmas clothes on.

living up to full potential. At the time, my mother was working as a nurse's aid at various hospitals, sometimes from 7 A.M. to 3 P.M., sometimes from 3 P.M. to 11 P.M., sometimes from 11 P.M. to 7 A.M., just wherever she was needed and whenever she could make the most money. Mother knew that things would be a whole lot easier for us if she were to move up out of the South. She was still going with Robert Lee at the time and he had people in Baltimore. So we up and moved

to Baltimore right before I was to start the second grade, right after I played the bear in our school play.

My cousins Sam and Diane were just so sad at my leaving. At that age my moving away to Baltimore seemed to them like I was moving away as far as the planet Mars. I'm a little older than they are and I taught them how to spell. The first word I taught them was *D-E-X-T-E-R*, so that they'd never forget me. Diane—me and her were favorite cousins. And little Sam? He was my favorite cousin too, and we are all still real, real close. When I left, Diane asked my mother, "Why do he have to leave?" You know it was like the circle was being broken. And me so far away! I made everybody make their children a promise, you know, "Our family'll go to Baltimore and visit Dexter and Carrie Emily once yearly." Sam and Diane came every year and I would go down to Athens various summers and stay the whole summer with 'em. To this day, they call me *D-E-X*.

I wasn't exactly scared to move to the big city so young, maybe just because I was too young to know better. Everything was so different from down in Georgia. We'd had a nice big apartment in Georgia, but this Baltimore house was the kind of house that's so small you open up the front door and trip over the back fence in one move. No grass in our new yard. In fact, we didn't have no kind of yard at all. Just a little white marble stoop in front of a row house covered in Formstone and with a little alleyway running behind. So no more mudpies and play greens. But there were other little boys to play with, like Ronnie and Greg, some of Robert Lee's nephews who were about my age.

I guess there's a bigger poverty range in the big cities of the North. You know the stuff you see there would spook you. Lower east side, New York. There you see everything. Raggedy buildings. Poverty. Hopelessness. Cars sitting on milk crates. Just the pits. I know people talk down the South but I have never seen living like I have seen in some of the big Northern cities, just nasty dirty and torn up. Also up

North they are really afraid to get much involved with folks, you know because they think everybody's out to get one another. Which is somewhat true. You know you hate to think like that but it's the real deal. It's someone always running some kind of con game. The only way the two places, South and North, are about equal is this. I heard my barber say one time, he said, "Everybody around here knows everybody else, so if somebody robs you for a quarter, they gotta go ahead and kill you 'cause they know you, went to school with your brother, played cards with your daddy, and dated your sister." And in the big cities they'd just as soon shoot you as look at you. So we're about equal.

My mother went up to Baltimore without me at first, to get a job and get situated. For safekeeping, she left me with her friend Miss Hannah, who lived in the Bottoms. In Athens there's a place called the Bottoms that's a shade shady. One day I looked out the front door and saw my Granddaddy Hamp going to the bootlegger next door. I cried out, "Granddaddy Hamp. It's me. Dexter!"

"Son, what are you doing in this house. Where's your mama?" he said.

When I explained, he bundled me up part and parcel and took me to live with him and Grandmama Francis. I stayed there about a week before I moved in with my father Bo Weaver and his wife Magnolia. I stayed with Bo and 'Nolia until Mother could come fetch me, about a year.

When I got there to Baltimore, believe me, Dexter was still country. Down here when we first lay eyes on you in the morning or on the street, we say "hey!" They do not do that in Baltimore, they say "hi." One time I was out with Robert Lee driving his handicap van and we stopped and Robert Lee said "hi" to a grandmother-type lady he knew. I said to her, "hey!" And she said to me, "Hay is for horses. I am not a horse." I could have disagreed with the lady on that point, but instead I was just real careful whenever I greeted somebody from then on. It took me a long time to adapt and understand the Northern accent because it's sort of up-tempo and all rapid-fire, whereas we-all down here think about what we say and let it stew awhile.

By me living in Baltimore for seventeen years and being accustomed to the Northern accent, it doesn't work the last nerve like it used to do. And now when I go to Baltimore they all like my Southern ways. They say, "Hey, let's hang out with Weaver D. He's country." And like any little thing I do or say, they'll just bust out laughing. I'll be saying to myself, "What's so funny?", but they'll be really tripping off me. They like to take me to parties and stuff and say, "Y'all, listen what he might say next."

As an adult I've noticed a lot of differences between the way we eat and the way people up North do. For one thing, they just never sit down to have a square meal, meat and three. They just eat sandwiches all the time, sandwiches,

sandwiches, sandwiches. But it might not even be healthy or well-balanced, because they are more into fast food there too. Just sandwiching it and hitting it, getting on the get-go. Since they walk all the time everywhere they go, around the city block, into the subway, out of the subway, to the stores, I would think they would need something more substantial.

I was visiting my friend Randy up North and I thought that he and his sandwiching friends would be real happy to have a cook staying with them. About suppertime when I first got there, or the day after, I stood up and thought I might make some little pork chops for my hosts. I looked up in the pantry and they had all this corn and French string beans and rice and such. So I caught myself cooking two or three of those vegetables to go with my chops and some sweet tea and whatnot. And if I'd served that meal to some people back home you would have seen the kind of eating where if you don't want your arms bit off, you keep your elbows off the table. But Randy and that Northern bunch didn't eat hardly anything. Just ate a sandwich and kept on walking. Their not eating hurt my feelings a little trifle, but my last Sunday there I still made steamed cabbage and a chuck roast and potatoes and carrots and cornbread. Because it doesn't matter where you are, *everyone* likes that for Sunday supper. Automatic.

The one thing about the North I got used to quick was the temperature change. We moved at the beginning of summer when in Georgia it can be a hundred degrees at 10 A.M. As children we would go in the house before noon and just lay around inside soaking up that sweet fan breeze and maybe venture out at three or four, after it cooled off somewhat. I used to always walk around barefooted in the summer and everyone would say, "You gonna have big feet if you go barefooted all the time." That's what they said and a lot of them wore shoes in the hottest of summer heat just for that reason. The only time I didn't go barefooted is when the sun beat down on the cement all day and got it hot as lava rock. You'd get a three-alarm burn. But compared to what I was used to, that first Baltimore summer was mild, mild.

Things had settled into a regular pattern by the time I went off to fourth grade in 1966. I was adjusting real well to living in the inner city. Life hadn't gotten so much easier for Mother yet, but living in a city with opportunity and with Robert Lee and his people gave us hope. I went to Public School #146 and had Miss Smith as my teacher. She was a pretty, brown-skinned woman who dressed very modest.

Of course, I have always loved learning and going to school. But Miss Smith had an extra bonus. You know, P.S. 146 had a lot of poor children from inner Baltimore city who really weren't eating breakfast. Maybe food wasn't so plentiful at home or maybe their parents just were asleep at the wheel. But Miss Smith saw the problem with these kids, that they couldn't hear the lesson over their stomachs growling and they were all the time making disruptions.

That's called being so poor you can't afford to pay attention. For real. So little Miss Smith instituted the big breakfast program for our class. That's when we had pancakes and bacon and those big Moore Park sausages they sell in Baltimore and eggs any way. We had one guy, I believe ate about thirteen pancakes. As a kid, that is a lot.

At P.S. 146 we didn't have a school cafeteria so we all had to bring those brown bag lunches. Back then lunch for a lot of the children was a welfare SPAM sandwich with a slice of brick-type cheese, you know those welfare SPAM and orange cheese sandwiches with a little skim coat of mayonnaise. When you took one of those canned meat sandwiches to P.S. 146, you'd have to hunker over and keep it all scrunched up in the Baggie and eat it as fast as you could swallow. If the other children caught wind of that sandwich, they'd all get around you: "Outta sight! A welfare SPAM sandwich!" Some of the ones making fun might have had a little mouth-watering too, because they'd developed a taste for that government SPAM at home. The kids even made up a blessing to say on lunch break: "Thank you, Lord, for the rice, the bread, and the peas. And thank you for the checks that we monthly receive." But some of the children I knew growing up might not have wanted the other children to see them brown bagging a welfare SPAM sandwich at all so they would flat-out not eat lunch, just ditch their brown bags on the way to school. So Miss Smith's breakfasts might be the only meal that those children ate all day long. That would make learning impossible. Some of Miss Smith's class was so poor they were eating banana sandwiches, ketchup sandwiches, sugar sandwiches. Put the sugar on the bread and call it *sandwich*.

In addition to me having my restaurant, I also manage an employee cafeteria at a manufacturing plant and sometimes people will come through the line and buy a banana and two slices of white bread on the side. I know that they're eyeballing those mayonnaise packets by the check-out. I know what they're doing, they're going to make them a banana sandwich. And I say, "Y'all are taking me *all* the way back. I just might have to eat myself a banana sandwich." With a little mayonnaise, slice those bananas up. *Mmm-hmm*. A banana sandwich is *good*.

I've always been very grateful that I had that foundation of a full stomach and caring teachers. If I hadn't gotten off on the good foot, hadn't had a mother who saw to it that I went to school everyday, hadn't had teachers who wanted to teach instead of just babysit, I don't know where I'd be today. You parents, keep Billy and Sally in school and get involved.

When I entered Miss Beatrice Payne's sixth grade in 1968, I already had my foundation built. I think Miss Payne could see that and she knew that she wanted to take me to the next level. Mother had always seen to it that I wore nice clothes, cleaned and pressed, and had good manners. Miss

Payne just took a shine to me. She saw a lot of capabilities and she probably though that one day I would succeed.

All of us were from apartments in the inner city, mostly the east-side ghetto was where we lived. Miss Payne had a three-story house all to herself on the west side. I guess it was two stories and then she had a basement. In the area Miss Payne lived at, ooh, the streets were so clean, no broken glass in the alley, like there was in the back alleys of where we lived. And you didn't see boarded-up houses in her block or none of that! She had a big painted cement porch and she had a front room in her house just for guests to sit down in. She had a big tropical aquarium where she raised guppies and those tropical fish. She also had an aquarium in the classroom and she would bring in a lot of her baby fishes from home. She gave me some too. She wanted us to see beyond the east-side ghetto, to her west side, and a little beyond.

Since we didn't have a school cafeteria sometimes a big group of us would walk to home together at noontime. Back then a real popular tennis shoe was out called Jack Purcell. They came with a white, black, or blue stripe across the toe and had the name Jack Purcell stamped on the back. That was when everyone on the east side learned to run—not because the shoes were so bouncy, but because you had to run unless you wanted your Jacks stolen off your two feet. That was around the time everyone was singing that song by Martha Reeves and Vandellas:

> Coming out around the world
> Are you ready for a brand new beat?
> Summer's here and the time is right
> For dancin' in the street.

Miss Payne was a church lady, a Baptist church lady. She dressed modest, like the Bible says to. At school she always wore those knee-covering skirts and a little sweater with a matching sweater over it, what was called a twin set, just in case she would get a chill or something in the classroom. And little earrings, pearls. Not the big dangly doorknocker kind. She had grayish hair, which she wore with a little part right here, in the nature of a bob. Miss Payne was a beautiful light brown, and I think her mother was biracial, she was telling me. Her mother had eleven children and she was from Virginia.

Several years ago, Miss Payne got me to drive her to Richmond, Virginia, to her hometown. We stayed at a cousin of her's house and we went to the church where she worshiped as a little girl. There was two Sanctified ladies there (you know I really liked them by me being Sanctified myself) and Miss Payne said, "They're always somewhere shouting and all." Miss Payne was totally Baptist and did not go in for a lot of shouting.

In Miss Payne's class every Friday we did Current Events as a part of our American History class. Some of Miss

Payne's favorite people were the Hunts, the Rockefellers, and the Kennedys, and Miss Payne loved to talk about Jacqueline Lee Bouvier Kennedy. She might start out talking about what President Kennedy had done when he was in the White House, but she'd always end up on Jackie, what Jackie was wearing, where Jackie went on vacation with her sister Lee or Mother Rose or Ethel, what little dresses she put on Caroline or what John John had done. I know Miss Payne knew her history, but she also wanted to expose us kids to other ways of life. Even if it was just through a clip from *Look* magazine.

My other favorite teacher at P.S. 146 was Miss Ruby Dudley. She always made sure that all her sixth graders had their notebooks and pencils, and that we kept a journal. If she asked a question and a child said he didn't know, Miss Payne would say, "Look in your treasure chest. Where is your treasure?" She would be so disappointed when a student did not have his answer written down or his thoughts in his journal, his treasure chest. Some of the kids thought that was real funny. Miss Dudley's treasure chest was nothing but a Big Chief notebook—just ruled paper and some scribble. There was no treasure chest in the ghetto. But I knew what Miss Dudley was talking about. I "made the connection" long before Oprah was telling me to.

One Friday morning in April, Miss Payne called us to Current Events. In our past lessons, students had gotten up to tell the class how the Reverend Dr. Martin Luther King

Jr. was planning a Poor People's March on Washington and was taking up the cause of the garbage workers who were on strike in Memphis. That week a little boy got up to talk about Dr. King, but not about the Poor People's March or the garbage workers.

He said, "Martin Luther King got killed last night."

The room was real quiet, but somebody from the back of that classroom at P.S. 146 said, clear as a bell, "Who is Martin Luther King?"

Miss Payne just turned around and stared. "You don't know who Martin Luther King is?" She looked like that little black child's not knowing or remembering, being alive and breathing in 1968 and being ignorant of this leader, was almost as big a crime as what happened to Martin himself. "You don't know who Martin Luther King is?" Miss Payne tried to show us currents events, what was happening in the world, who was important, but sometimes children just didn't get engaged with what was going on. How can anyone walk through such a world of riches as ours and have their own treasure chest be empty?

Like I said, Miss Payne took a shine to me and wanted to expose me to as much culture as she could. We spent a lot of time talking after class and I spent several weekends with her. On Friday afternoons, we'd pile in the car with Miss White, my fifth grade teacher. She always drove Miss Payne to work because she lived nearby and Miss Payne didn't drive. Like is customary in some people's homes, on Friday nights Miss Payne would always eat fish for dinner. Not because she was Catholic, she just liked fish.

By now you know Weaver D has always liked to get his food on. One Friday night we were having dinner with some of her neighborhood friends, ministers and teachers and all, at Miss Payne's. I was eating that fish like it was going out of style. I was a couple of plates into it, when one of Miss Payne's friends said, "Son, if I were your relation I think I'd rather clothe you than feed you."

Miss Payne and I'd go to different places, museums and outings and such. She got me and friends of mine involved in campaigning for Clarence Mitchell III who was running for city council in her district. We stood out on the corner and passed out leaflets and told everybody "Vote for Clarence Mitchell III," and different things like that.

One time Miss Payne's sister Florence got real, real sick and she needed some blood so Miss Payne told me, "Dexter, I want you to give some blood for my sister and I want you to find some of your friends who will also give. And each one of 'em I'll give twenty dollars to." Boy, I roused up a whole lot of children who wanted to give their blood to Miss Payne, way more people than the twenty-dollar blood she needed. My friend Big Ann wanted to donate and she weighed about four hundred pounds so we all thought she'd be ripe for a *lot* of good blood. But after they stuck her a couple of times they couldn't find a decent vein. Miss Payne gave her the twenty dollars anyway.

Miss Payne had her own piano and I was allowed to prac-
tice on it whenever I cared to. Just any little thing like that
that Miss Payne could do for me, she was all the time doing.

But don't think that because I was teacher's pet, and I was,
that I got any special privilege. Miss Payne named me to
P.S. 146's Model United Nations. We were going to take a
trip to Washington, D.C., to delegate with Andrew Young,
who was the real UN ambassador at the time. Well, teacher's
pet cut up in class, I don't remember to this day what I did,
and Miss Payne made sure that I followed the rules just like
everyone else. I didn't get to go to Washington, D.C., or to
delegate with Andrew Young. I lost the privilege.

We stayed close for years after I left school. In 1976 when
I was still living in Baltimore I wanted to come to my family
reunion. I called her and said, "Miss Payne, I want to go to
my family reunion in Atlanta, Georgia."

She said, "You do?"

"Yes ma'am, I do but I don't have any money."

So she said, "OK, I'm gonna loan you fifty dollars for a
Greyhound bus ticket to Georgia." And she gave me the
fifty dollars and she said, "You can just pay me back the way
you want to."

As soon as I could after the Weaver reunion, I started paying her back in dribs and drabs. I think after I paid her
maybe twenty or thirty of the dollars back she said, "That's
all right. You don't have to pay back the rest. I just wanted

to teach you how to pay back somebody who's loaned you some money. You should pay them back in a certain way. I just wanted to teach you that lesson."

So that's a lesson I try with young people myself. If they say, "Loan me something," and I see that they have real good grades, are really trying, I'll loan it to them, and then when they come to pay me back I say to myself, "Ahh, they paying it back." Like that. Then with that last payment or so I just say, "Don't worry about it. I'm glad to be able to help you." Or something like that. "Keep the good work up."

Yeah, Miss Payne's still alive, way up in her nineties. Her birthday is the twenty-ninth of November and mine is the twenty-eighth. She still lives in the same house in the same neighborhood and it's still holding. I can remember her phone number off the top of my head.

THIRTY-FIVE CENTS A SHINE

◆ 4 ◆

When you did The Bump with
big Susie, you **stayed**
bumped.

→**MOTHER** always says, "Dexter, one thing about you, you have always seen me work and that's all you do is work. But if I was a woman sitting around on the welfare, then you'd be sitting around lazy too, 'cause you know it breeds that kind of stuff." When I was in junior high and high school, I saw Mother go off to work every day as a nurse's aid at Baltimore City Hospital, which is now Johns Hopkins Bayview Medical Center. I have always had a good work ethic and it all goes back to that.

My mother made a statement one time, she said, "You look at the projects and there is generation after generation there." A friend of mine lived in the Flagg projects in Baltimore. Me and him were best buddies. He still lives in Flagg projects, his sister lives in Flagg projects, his brother lives in Flagg projects. They all live in Flagg projects. Mother was right.

I've always seen how important it is to make your own. In high school a big group of us would hang at the rec center across the street from where I lived, then we'd go off to the sweet shop or the hamburger stand. Nobody but me worked, so they were always broke. This one would be biting off my hamburger. This other one would be saying, "You gonna eat those pickles?" Of course, I'd have to be "sharing" my fries. And the other ones would be passing around my drink cup like it was a wampum peace pipe. These are the people Miss Dudley always would be getting upset about because their treasure chests were empty. No pencils, no notebooks. No after-school jobs, no money. No college degree, no career. It all starts when you're knee-high.

Those people who don't want to turn their hand at work think they are free. But when my friend from the Flagg projects came to visit me at my house, the other children in my neighborhood would all the time be asking me, "Uh, don't he have to go back home soon, 'fore the gate close?"

I try to inspire the people who work for me to go out and achieve and do their dream. But sometimes, it makes me mad, not only do they just not have the foundation of good habits, but they're thinking about how they can slip one over on the world. I used to use this term, that if a person hasn't done anything by age twenty-five, they're not gonna do anything. And I told this one guy that one time.

He said, "Ooh, I'm 24, I got one more year."

Mother worked as a medical aide at North Charles General Hospital for two years until there were openings at the practical nursing school at City Hospital. She went to school during the day and worked at NCGH nights and weekends. She took her board tests and, at age thirty-four, she became a licensed practical nurse. She went back to school at forty-two to Community College of Baltimore—now it's called Baltimore City Community College—and became a registered nurse. She even went on to get a bachelor's degree in social work— she graduated in the top ten per cent of her class!

I've learned a lot from my mother. Now that I'm in business and dealing with employees, some things I take for granted, like how my mother used to tell me to dress nice and how she told me to be clean. She taught me that people look at you from your head to your toe so if you've got runned-over shoes, rat's-nest hair, somebody's going to see it. People come to me looking for a job and I'm thinking, "Hey, you want to be working in food service and you're looking like that?" Oh yeah. You find folks in food service all the time fiddling with some piece of metal poked in their face, the nose ring, the lip ring, the *eyebrow* ring. Looks to me like folks should be worrying more about earning a golden ring, you know I mean a *halo*, around their head than some old trinket they get from the Hoochie Store for $1.99.

I went to the doughnut shop one morning and the lady there was just working her nose ring like a set of worry beads and she says, "Uh . . . duh, which ones you want?" And I'm like "*Ooh*." I'm thinking that that same nasty hand is gonna be picking up my six jellies, three glazed, and three assorted, you know what I mean. And I'm like, "Oh, I'm gonna pass. You have a nice day!"

Sometimes I see a caterer and he's run down, tore up, teeth all rotten, and you don't know whether you want to eat that food or not. But I feel as though I look the part. 'Cause every job is part the acting thing too. You have got to say, "I am here. I look good. I work good. Eat my food and pay me." Every day I am in business, so every day I have to look like I am ready, willing, and able to work. Some people leave their house looking like they are fleeing from a fire!

And another thing you see with the people, they might not have any dress clothes. Now I find out the average young person doesn't even have a set of dress clothes, and if someone died in their family they'd have to go downtown and buy a set of clothes or borrow some from a cousin. I was taught in business seminars that everybody should have some business wear, women need a navy blue skirt and coat suit, and men should have a dark jacket, blue, black, or gray, you know, the three business colors.

There are some people who just need an attitude makeover. I'm not one of these types who wants everyone to know about every piece of silverware ever made, how to navigate through a set of silverware that has more blades than a surgeon's tray. I'm just asking you to say "thank you" and "please" when it's called for. When an employee takes money from a customer he should say "thank you," 'cause some of those ducats are goin' in his own hip pocket. Now come on! "May I help you, *please?*" Even if your little town only has two restaurants, there has to be a reason why that customer has crossed the threshold of *your* restaurant and not gone to the eats down the street. So say "please."

And another thing. One thing that gets to Weaver is when you're talking to someone and they're not giving any type response. I have had employees that I speak to and then I have to ask, "Did you hear me?"

"I heard you, I just didn't say nothing."

Didn't say nothing? You are ignoring me! Do not put the ig on me and leave me talking to myself! That will send me through the roof. And the young people are famous for putting the ig on you. It used to be, my mother said, that my little half-sister that is nineteen months younger than me, you'd be telling her something and she'd ig you, she'd put an ig on you that wouldn't wait. Maybe that's where I developed the aversion.

And my second most pet peeve is when somebody *does* respond to you and they're huffing, "I'm coming! I'm coming!"

They taught us in fast food management—hey, chicken will be ready in three minutes, five minutes, four minutes, you let the customer know minutes. "OK, it'll be ready in this many minutes." When somebody told Miss Payne "I'm coming!", she would say, "Christmas is coming on December twenty-fifth. *When* are *you* coming?"

I just think that you have to have pride about yourself always, be clean and know how to act. No matter how bad you might be feeling, you might not have a dime in your pocket, you might not have anything in your refrigerator, but you hold your head up, nobody will know it. My grandmama, I look at her for this too. She taught me to walk tall and straight, with the head up. (Everybody that meets my grandmama, she's eighty-one years old, says, "Ooh, that little lady . . . she got a lot on the ball." 'Cause she'll tell you in a minute, "If you got a man, honey, don't let him put his shoes under your bed. Put them on the outside of the door. Put them under your bed, you never will get rid of 'em. Like a dog that sprays." She has a lot to teach.)

Just as soon as I could, in junior high school or thereabouts, I started working around the block for my nickels and pennies. In the springtime I would sell carnation corsages all around the neighborhood so that the ladies could have them for Mother's Day or whatever day. Corsages for the ladies, and buds for the men. They wore white if their mothers were dead and red if they was still living. I also went door to door and sold mixed boxes of Cheerful House greeting cards from samples. One box of two dozen of the various Cheerful House cards would get you through a whole lifespan, from "It's a Boy" and "Your First Communion"; to "So, You Graduated," "On Your Wedding Day," and "Your First Baby"; and all the "Happy Birthday" and "Merry Christmas" cards you would need, 'til you use up that last "Get Well Soon" and hit the "Dear Bereaved." I sold garden seeds for people who had a little plot of carrots and beans and cabbage between their house and the alley, toothbrushes, seven-year light bulbs. Everybody uses toothbrushes and light bulbs. I also made a killing on the *Gospel News Journal*. Each month they would feature a different gospel artist, and I remember Clara Ward was on the cover one month, and The Mighty Clouds of Joy was on another month. And I would go to the big gospel concerts around Baltimore and sell them. What didn't I sell?

If I was in Baltimore for the summer, me and my cousin Jerry would see what kind of pocket change we could pick up in the neighborhood. We were too young to get workers permits. Back then you had to be about fifteen years old to get a workers permit. In summer we would race up to the ambulance company every day and see who could be the first to wash the ambulance or pick up glass in the alley. It was good money. In winter we would shovel snow for senior citizens or take people's clothes to and from the cleaners.

Along about junior high Mother and I moved to Montpelier Street, next door to Thelma Lee. Thelma's husband was a member of the Grant Specials gospel group. They sang at Southern Baptist events and they had a 45 out, you know, one of those 45 rpm records, the little singles with the big hole in the middle, and on one side of the Grant Specials's 45 is "Give Me All My Flowers." You might've heard that old song, "Give me my flowers so I can see them / And I can enjoy the beauty that they bring." Don't wait 'til I'm dead and have a whole truckload behind me, that's the significance of it. And on the flip side was "There's a Leak in this Old Building."

There is no other way to say it, Thelma was *big*. A big, beautiful woman. And she would go around the house all day singing, "There's a leak in this old building, and my soul has got to *move*." You know, we'd hear Thelma starting up next door and Mother and I would say, "O Lord!" For real. So she'd play that big Grant Specials song "Give Me All My Flowers" on the hi-fi about twenty times and then she'd flip it over and work the B-side about another twenty times. "There's a Leak in this Old Building," that B-side was called.

Thelma loved her some gospel music. She and I were at Sister Williams's house on Montpelier Street one day and they had an electric organ and we were just praising God and everything and Thelma was all in the spirit. Thelma got up and was hopping on one foot and then the other, just feeling the spirit and *testifying*. She lost her balance on one of those good hops and knocked everybody to the wall.

Thelma might have been feeling the power of the Lord, but the rest of us were feeling the power of Thelma.

Thelma could smell what my mother was cooking through the walls of those row houses. I mean to say that sweet woman was like one of those drug-sniffing dogs who work at the airport. Soon as Mother would put on a good pot of beans, we'd hear a knock-knock-knock on the wall.

"Carrie, what you got over there that's good to eat? You gonna give me some of them pinto beans? I smell 'em."

One Christmas Mother got the turkey stuffed and dressed and in the oven before she had to leave for work for the day. Thelma came over to "keep an eye on it." Well, she tasted that stuffing every five minutes and by the time the bird was brown she had entirely *un*stuffed it. Mother got home and took one look up inside that hollow, empty bird and she said, "D, tell me what Thelma has done!"

I was real good friends with her kids, especially her son LoLo. LoLo was the first to get the idea to sell the *Afro-American News*, but he could never quite sell as many as he should. By this time, I had been a greeting card salesman, a garden seed salesman, a seven-year lightbulb salesman, so I told LoLo how he could make some money. We would stand out in front of all the big churches each Sunday and go up and down the aisles of the gospel shows. We would make a killing at those gospel shows. And the people would see we were good boys and would want to support us, they even asked for us by name.

LoLo also took me to a new kind of store in the neighborhood, a co-op. They have them still today, but in the sixties they were real popular. Members of the co-op pooled their money all together in a pot and bought bulk, bulk, bulk. Bulk soybean and bulk carrots and bulk macaroni. And then they would sell it to people at a discount if they were a member of that organic kick.

This was the time when I was first introduced to people of all different types, light-skinned, dark-skinned, white, multiracial, and those that didn't eat meat. They ate a lot of cheeses, soybeans, and all kind of stuff that was natural and organic. Pumpkin seeds and pistachio nuts and sunflower seeds. The co-op folks didn't check to see if I had a workers permit, so I was able to work at that hippie co-op like an adult. I would weigh all that bulk stuff on the scale, slice up different kinds of cheeses for the people, give change, and take orders over the phone. That's how I was first introduced to that cheese called Muenster cheese.

I enjoyed working at that coop. But D has to have something of his own on the side, so I made cupcakes and cakes and stuff at home in my mother's oven and sold them at the co-op. Those hungry hippies bought those in bulk too.

Robert Lee had seen me for years going around the block trying to line my pocket with money from the Cheerful House cards, the *Gospel Music News,* and the seven-year lightbulbs, and he was real supportive of little Dexter's work ethic. My first year at Woodbourne Junior High School in 1969, Robert Lee made me a shoeshine box. It was made of scrap wood and the slat for the foot rest was already painted black when we found it! I had all my rags, saddle soap, Meltonian and Kiwi polishes, edge dressings, and brushes hard and soft, in one place. Oh, and an old toothbrush to work the grooves. Automatic.

Looking so innocent, this was during my shoeshine days and all the MLK riots

So I set off—a happy little entrepreneur—to go find the perfect spot to set up my shoeshine box. Until you go into the shine business you never notice how many people walk around in shoes that need to be either retreaded or retired.

I staked out my box on Lafayette Avenue and on street corners all around the east side. Lots of the buildings on North Avenue had been looted and even burned during the MLK riots and were never replaced. There were still buildings there with broken-out storefront windows, with big

pieces of dirty plate glass hanging from the frames, looking like the teeth of a wild dog. There were buildings, used to be grocery stores and dress shops, so covered with soot they looked like someone had covered them with tar. After the riots, folks were afraid to rebuild their family businesses there and a lot of liquor stores and pool halls opened up. Many of the businesses that weren't burnt down during the riots were the bars. A little kid trying not to be scared around all these broke-down buildings with teeth, I would set up my shoeshine box on a corner under a streetlight. Like Lady Day sang it, "God help the child that got his own."

I liked to set up shop in front of The 19th Hole or another bar called J.B.'s. My business was not a drive-thru, it was a walk-thru. The men would stop on their way into a club because they wanted to look like a player, or they would get a shine as they were leaving a club because they were feeling beer-generous. I charged thirty-five cents for the best shine in Baltimore but on payday some men would kindly tip me sixty-five cents to make it an even dollar.

We listened mostly to gospel music at home and working on those street corners is where I heard a lot of that good sixties music, *my* sixties music, for the first time. When the doors to the 19th Hole or J.B.'s would swing open I heard it all: The Supremes's "You Can't Hurry Love," The Four Tops's "Standing in the Shadow of Love," plus The Jackson Five, The Three Degrees, The Staple Singers.

Doesn't sound like much, but I gave shines for about a year and it's hard to tell how much money I made, thirty-five cents a pop. I had my own bank account. For real.

Some of the best times me and Robert Lee spent together was when I was in those junior high years and we would drive down to Georgia to visit the Weavers and the Eberharts in the summertime. Those summers back in Georgia were great for a boy.

I have cousins named Jennifer and Frederick. They were somewhat near my age, and I played with them. The three of us always paid visits to Grandmama Frances in Bishop. We walked barefooted a lot and helped her in the garden. I remember my grandmother had a garden with sweet potatoes, green beans, corn, just plenty of everything you would want to eat. We were always eating those tomatoes right off the vine, still warm from the sun and sprinkled with salt. I remember it got to where I wouldn't go to the garden without Grandmama Frances's salt shaker in my pocket.

And I remember a lot of love. Looks like to me the further down South you go the more lovable the old people are. And my grandmother was from Greene County, Georgia, *way* on down South.

One time she was saying, I was about thirty-one or somewhere around like that at the time, she said, "Dexter, you still a baby." With a grandmother, you never grow up. She said, "I'm the oldest one in the family and y'all are still all children." Now that's the best combination: to have someone respect you as an adult, but want to care for and love you like a child. And that is what grandmothers do.

From those earliest times of selling door to door and giving shines in front of The 19th Hole and J.B.'s, I saved and saved. But I'm not one of those who is as tight as the bark on a tree—I've always been sure to reward myself and give myself some of the finer things in life. If we got good marks all the junior-high schoolers in Baltimore could get free entry on Report Card Day to Gwynn Oak Amusement Park, but I was able to go pretty often on my own in spring and summer, paying my own way. Most of my friends couldn't afford to get in, so I'd spot them a couple of dollars and off we'd go on the #28 bus for a day of red hots and spook houses. Later on, I could afford things like the designer jeans outfits and platform shoes that all the kids wanted but couldn't afford. I still remember the time I hopped on one of those mint green-and-white Baltimore Transit Company buses, one of the old-school city buses shaped like a loaf of bread, to Montgomery Ward and made a beeline for that electronics department. I put down cash for a little color TV, probably the first on our block. For years I kept that little rabbit-eared TV on a metal stand in my bedroom and was just so proud. I also took little trips with church groups and with friends and their parents. I could always go on my own and pay for my own and that always made me real proud.

I think all parents ought to get their children to work around fifteen, sixteen, seventeen, even if it's no more than baggin' it at the Piggly Wiggly. It helps the child get the feel of money, his own and his parents' too. I think that working children get a good money sense when they learn that one Nintendo game costs this many hours' worth of wearing a paper hat at the drive-thru, or costs this week's worth of asking "Paper or plastic?"

Every day here in Athens, you see these kids in college at the University of Georgia in big Jeeps and four-wheel SUVs and foreign cars. I know it must feel good for parents to give their kids a nice new car. But I have to wonder what they are taking away with one hand as they are giving with the other.

There was a lot of pressure on us kids to quit school back in the seventies when I was at Mergenthaler Vocational Technical High School. Back in the day you could drop out of school when you were sixteen and there were those who counted down to the sweet sixteen like they were being released from Cellblock C. Those who had dropped out before would always be coming around saying this and that about how only chumps would be in the classroom. Some who worked at Bethlehem Steel in Baltimore County would come around telling tales of how much money they were making. Everybody who had a job smelting at Bethlehem Steel thought they could retire from there. Now I wonder where all those one-time children are.

I'd worked hard in the classroom and at the commercial baking work-study program at Mervo and at the after-school job I had working as an orderly at the same nursing home where my mother was an LPN. In gym class that year,

I got my nickname Weaver D. We had a big old gym class at Mervo, so the teacher had to call roll by name and number. I was "Weaver, D.: 43." Kind of sing-song and before long it got shortened just to Weaver D. Now when anybody calls me Dexter, I look around—where's the Dexter at?

A lot of my friends resisted all the temptations to drop out. I was looking forward to all that the world had to offer Weaver. So I thought to myself that I am going to give myself and all those Mergenthaler Vocational-Technical High School seniors the biggest graduation party that this block of Alameda Avenue has ever seen!

Our pomp and circumstance was at the Baltimore Civic Center. I ran around to all the graduating Mervo seniors as they were standing in line to take their seats, the girls still bobby-pinning their mortarboards on and the boys shining the tops of their shoes on the back of their pants, and I handed out invitations to everyone, forty in all.

I'd spent the three days before commencement in the kitchen making all the food. I roasted chickens and made a big bowl of Grandmama Rena's potato salad and whipped up some cole slaw. I gave an older senior the cash to buy some pure grain alcohol, to put some punch in the punch.

And I had to look cute for my own party so I went out and bought some short white pants and Jesus sandals. Back then they wore what was called a penny-ribbed shirt, you remember those? So I had on white shorts and sandals and a penny-ribbed shirt and it was real special.

I had to get the music together to play on our big console stereo. I Scotch-taped a copper penny to the arm of the stereo so that the needle wouldn't skip when the dancing got to rocking the house. I knew all the seniors would want to hear "We the People" by The Staple Singers. Don Cornelius had just started playing it on *Soul Train* and it was sort of like our Class of 1974 song. "We the Seniors" is how we hit it. And "Dancing Machine" by The Jackson Five. "When Will I See You Again" by The Three Degrees. There was "Rock the Boat" by The Hues Corporation: "Rock the boat. Don't rock the boat, baby." Mother said to push all the good furniture against the walls and roll up the carpet. Mother knew it was going to be a PARTY!!!

So we had the graduation ceremony and all the girls were crying like they're so happy to be leaving those four walls when really they're scared about what's on the other side, and all the boys were punching each other on the arm pretending like they're not nervous to be leaving the nest. I was just thinking about those big bowls of potato salad and all that hi-test punch back home in our harvest gold Kelvinator. I headed home right after the ceremony, and there were already five or ten hungry-looking people waiting on the stoop, looking like orphans dropped off at a foundling home. Now I had only invited the graduating seniors, but what showed up that night was the *tenth* graders, the *eleventh* graders, the *twelfth* graders, the drop-*outs*, and a few drop-*ins* besides. And it wasn't just students from

Mergenthaler, there were Lake Clifton H.S. people and Northwestern H.S. people and City College H.S. people there too. It seemed like everybody who had ever attended a Baltimore City school, or anybody who'd ever driven through a school zone, was thinking they were invited.

Phyllis Johnson—me and her were good friends from our commercial baking classes—and all her sisters came. I think she must have been one of those who went all over saying, "Dexter Weaver is having a party, y'all." Phyllis's mother was Mother Johnson who was a holy mother. When Phyllis and I first met, she went on to tell Mother Johnson about that she had this boy in her class that was saved and his name was Dexter Weaver, and Mother Johnson said, "Ooh, I want to meet him!" So I went on to Phyllis Johnson's house one day and met Mother Johnson and met her other daughters and all, and they all liked me, so when I had a party they knew they all could come. And Phyllis was a big dancer at the graduation party.

Karon, next-door Thelma's daughter, tried to hit that punched-up punch like her mama did. But Thelma was a big girl and there was no keeping up with her. Poor Karon could barely stand up the next day when she went to another school's prom. They almost didn't get her picture took for all the stomach upset.

My white friend named Susie was there. Susie was a healthy girl, a big healthy girl who was giving you gigantic butt. And just because she was a brick house does not mean that that blue-eyed soul sister didn't like to wear those little seventies halters and skinny cigarette-leg jeans. Nineteen seventy-four was the year they brought out The Bump. And just in time too because that dance was *invented* for a big girl like Susie. The girl could give you a bump to knock the gold caps off your teeth. Yes, when big-butted Susie bumped you, you *stayed* bumped. I think she was, like my friend Evangelist Diggs said, *in* the world. Susie and her Hustle was the first one on the floor and the last one to get off. That was the way Susie did. She opened a party and she closed it.

Word spread throughout the neighborhood that Weaver D's was the party to be at. So everybody filed out of all the graduation parties all over Baltimore and made their way to Weaver's. The little bit of pure grain I had kept everybody going all night long, just like in the Bible where the lady goes to the barrel to get more meal and no matter how many times she goes there's always more and more grain. We lived in a small place at the Kennedy Apartments and the party people were bustin' moves all up the stairway, all over the parking lot, just all over. It was so packed that after a while people couldn't have left if they'd wanted to. One guy was trying to leave and I guess he couldn't get through to the front door, so he tried crawling out the basement window. Mother lit in on him: "Oh no you *won't* crawl out of my window!" And next thing you know she's pulling him back in by his ankles. "You're leaving all right, but you're leaving through the front door like a civilized person." So

Mother pulled that poor boy back in the apartment just to make him leave.

That graduate party—the party I bought and paid for all myself—was a great send-off to all my school years. I learned how to work hard—in school and in a job—and to save and spend like I had good sense. Moving on and up step by step. And those are lessons I've used in everything I've ever done. Have you learned them too?

GOVERNMENT CHEESE

✦5✦

**Sell a quality product. Ever heard
of somebody losing money
selling pig ear and mustard
sandwiches?
Of course you haven't!**

→**THERE** had been some hard times during those teenage
years. Don't think there weren't. I bought myself some lux-
uries and trinkets with the money I made from selling my
wares, but sometimes I had to contribute to the running of
the household too. That's just the way the world worked
and I was glad to do it.

I've told you about Robert Lee and all the good things
about that man. But I also need to tell you some of the not-
so-good things. Robert Lee liked the dice and playing poker

and sometimes he lost all his check by gambling, so sometimes there was no food in the house. In those days one hundred gallons of heating oil cost nineteen dollars payable at delivery and, electric being cheaper and payable later, there were times we had to prop open the door of our electric stove to heat the house.

Senior picture from Mervo.
That's an Afro wig, you know.

But I'm thankful to have seen that, to have seen Robert Lee and his cronies in their floating card party get involved in all that mess. I knew from seeing that, even at a young age, that I never wanted to be a gambler. Now, sometimes I played, you know, I used to just play a little pitty pat for nickel bets. Pitty pat's a very beginning little card game most children learn how to play. But Robert Lee and them never played that. They played things like five-card stud and spades and pinochle. They were more into those. I don't even really know how all those games go, to tell you the truth. I guess I wanted that whole thing to be taken away from me. The only thing I remember from watching those games in our house is seeing the fear that those men felt, fear of making that next hand, fear of the first loss, fear of "can I make back the pot?", fear of the wife and of the rent man and of being hungry and of having children go hungry.

Don't forget Robert Lee had bad multiple sclerosis and, you see, he really couldn't work because of it. He got a check which they would call welfare back then. Later on, Robert Lee was upgraded to Federal Supplemental Income because of his MS being more crippling and he was able to get a little more money. And that was all the money he had, to save or to lose. And some of the time he made that second choice, the bad choice.

He was eligible to get dried beans, SPAM, and cheese and those stores always came in handy, gambling losses or not. For real. There were more than a few people in our neighborhood who fed their families with that Uncle Sam-brand cheese. At recess, the girls jumping double Dutch jump rope would sing, "We can tell by those knees—you been eating government cheese."

Double Dutch was one of the games back in the day. That and playing the dirty dozens. Do you know what that is? That's snappin' somebody, or usually somebody's mama, about being broke, or having bad hair, or being nasty. It may sound mean, but since everybody was in the same boat, we knew nobody was serious. Its really just a game to let off steam and see who is the quickest to talk the talk. Like you say to me, "Your mama so dumb it takes her an hour to cook

Minute Rice." And I say, "But at least my mama is not broke. *Your mama* is so broke her food stamps bounced." Then you come back with, "Yeah, your mama sure knows about food. *Your mama* is so big, when she stands on the corner, the cops say, 'Hey y'all, break it up!'" And on like that 'til one of us snaps something so funny and exaggerated we *both* of us start laughing.

When he was young Robert Lee had done a little shade shady this and that. All little kind of stuff. He was famous for the jailhouse. With nobody to come home to, he didn't care where he called home. That was one of the reasons he and Mother wanted to go to Baltimore. I guess he needed a change and when he moved to Baltimore with us, when he felt he had a family and everything, he never went back to jail.

Yeah, having Mother and me sort of changed his life. Robert Lee took me in as his son and never treated me otherwise. Even his sister Fanny Maud Mosby treated me like she was my aunt and all those Eberhardts became my family as if we'd shared blood. In Robert Lee's obituary printed up in the *Baltimore Sun*, Fanny Maud and them included me as a survivor because they knew that's what Robert Lee would have wanted.

By now you know me well enough to know that D is going to make the best of the hand he's been dealt and see if there is not a few honest ducats to be shaken out of a given situation. So instead of losing money at these floating poker and pinochle games of Robert Lee's, I made money by catering them. Those card parties would go around, rotate between all the houses of all the players—this week at Joe's house, next week at Buddy's, the week after at our house. And those times that Robert Lee hosted, I'd make a big pot of chitlins or pigs feet and sell them for a dollar a plate. I might do a little potato salad side dish and pass around the hot sauce. Sometimes I'd sell highball set-ups and Robert Lee would sell shots. Whenever Robert Lee would go back down South he would pick up some of that mountain liquor, what they call white lightening, moonshine. They also used to drink Johnny Walker Red and VO, I think it's

Joretta Pfieffer and me at Joretta's Lake Clifton High School prom.

called that. It's a bourbon or a brandy. Anyway, VO was the name of it and they used to really drink that VO. Robert Lee's brother-in-law Jerome Mosby used to always drink Johnny Walker Red.

So here were all these grown-up men, talking rough and drinking tough, and losing money hand over fist. And little

Weaver, just in junior high, was making his a little by little. Of course, somebody would always go away with a big win and some would drag home to a month of empty cupboards. Those guys were so busy tracking numbers and minding the pot they never noticed that Weaver was just going around real quiet collecting a dollar a pig ear sandwich here and fifty cents for a set-up there. Have you ever heard of somebody *losing* money selling pig ear and mustard sandwiches? I didn't think so! I never made a big till, but I never lost a dime either.

COME OUT OF THAT COMA!

◆6◆

Greens are good for you, but it's the drippings that make you want to eat 'em. Taste life!

◆EVANGELIZING is something born in you. I didn't take the pulpit until 1976 when I preached the word at Way of the Cross Apostolic Church in Baltimore, but I had been in the church all my life. I was filled with the Holy Ghost in 1959 at around the time the great-grandmother I told you about, Great-grandmama Emily, was in her sickbed. Seeing that woman face all the tests of pain and fear the Lord was throwing her way and seeing her hang on with faith all along, was all the proof anyone would need that God is in His Heaven. Even a child could see the power moving.

Well, I was born a Methodist. My mother and them used to go to the Methodist church, so as a little child I went to that church, but my dad, Bo Weaver, was Baptist and those times that I stayed down here in Athens with him, I went to Hill Chapel Baptist Church with Bo and the Weavers.

It was Robert Lee's mother who introduced me to Holiness in 1971. When I was six years old I went to a Sanctified church with Robert Lee's mother Viola, Sister Viola Eberhart, and I've been Sanctified since I hit that door. Sister Viola was strict Sanctified. Don't forget some of those Eberharts got put out 'cause they didn't want to abide by the strict teachings of Holiness. It's a strict faith. Lots of rules. Some people call it a "clothesline religion," because there are all kinds of rules about what kind of clothes the church women can wear, the length of hemlines, whether they can wear open-toe shoes or makeup, that kind of stuff. And some of those Sanctified people turn sixteen and they say, "I ain't going back to that church." It's so much like a bondage to them. Sanctified does not what you call *draw* many young adults. But at that real young age I loved to go to church, looked forward to it.

I can remember one Sunday walking from where Robert Lee's mother lived on Rocksprings Road up to St. John's Holiness, just Sister Viola and Aunt Ella—she was Sanctified and full of the Holy Ghost—and me, along with a few other church ladies I'd been quick to adopt as aunties. And see what it was, as a child I was happy to go because it was always excitement and the ladies in their church hats and people shouting and praising God, and I loved that almost as much as I loved the Lord. (Now some of the children don't respond to that and they get too riled up. You know how proper Miss Payne was, we already met her. But when she was a little girl in Virginia she and her sisters, all just as prim as she was, went to a Sanctified church and they were laughing at the people because of their holy rolling and the deacons put them out of that church. I mean to say *put them out.* How hard does a gaggle of little girls, in their Mary Jane shoes and knee socks, have to hee-haw before they get put out—PUT OUT—of church?)

Sanctified is nothing like this new trend of today. Just look at Bobby Jones and them, this new moderate gospel. And all this new Kurt Franklin, all this dancing and sequins and all. Look at Bobby Jones, with those back-up sisters all painted up, faces like they been dipped in cake batter. On TV doing all that sort of dance they used to do in the world. I don't come from that school. Maybe I'll have to grow to that. All I know is Shirley Caesar and The Caravans; Dorothy Norwood; Albertina Walker; The Five Blind Boys, a quintet out of Augusta, Georgia; groups like that.

But I don't know, because like I was saying, some of the old Holiness churches that didn't do this and didn't do that, they really don't have a lot of members now. I go around to some of the old churches that I used to evangelize at and they just have a handful of members and all of those are old mothers eighty- or ninety-something years old.

I was baptized as a child at St. John's Holiness Church and later on I was baptized again in Jesus' name by Bishop Canady at Refuge Way of the Cross Church. One thing about those Jesus-only churches, they'll baptize you right there if you say you want to, right there in the church. 'Cause what it is, they're trying to get that three godhead out of you—that Father, Son, and Holy Ghost—and if you are Baptist or Church of God in Christ or whatever they extend the invitation and say "if someone wants to join, come in and be baptized, the members are ready, the minister is ready, the pool is ready." They keep a spare robe ready to baptize you right then and there in the name of Jesus only.

You will hear different pastors on the radio fighting all the time about baptism. An elder from Church of God in Christ will say, "You must be baptized in the Father, Son, and Holy Ghost," then a Jesus-only elder will say, "You gotta be baptized solely in the name of Jesus." Me, I'm baptized in the Father, Son, and Holy Ghost *and* I'm baptized in the name of Jesus only. I'm covered both ways. Whatever the Lord is calling for, Weaver is covered. Amen and automatic.

If you are Sanctified or know someone who is, you now that those services are long, long, long, and some people are just not down with that. Once I told my mother and my aunts, "Ooh, my good friend from Baltimore is driving down to Athens for a revival," and my mother said she'd come and all my aunts said they would come to hear the Word too. And my friend preached the Word until night came on. Hours after dark she said, "Let us now take the linen off of God." And my aunt said, "My *Lord!* It's eleven o'clock and she's just now getting ready to take the linen off of Him! Well, I might need those linens myself 'cause I did not bring my nightgown this evening!" And, of course, just your regular service might take up at eleven in the morning and might not let you get out 'til about two or three in the afternoon.

You might say that those long services just eat up your Sunday and you *need* a day of rest. Even the Lord rested on the seventh day. But you see if you are saved you *want* to hear the Word. You want to get among the saints 'cause a lot of them testify and say, "I thank God for being in the house of the Lord. I know my inheritance is among the Sanctified." You *want* to be among the Sanctified. So being in those long services is like a rest—better than laying flat out on the sofa with the clicker at your left hand and a PBR at your right— because it gives you the ultimate peace of mind and all the struggles of the week are put on the shelf. Church is a day of rest.

Part of being in the church is getting to go to all the good church dinners. I have been to I don't know how many in I don't know how many churches. All the ladies bring whatever they're famous for—their red velvet cake or their secret family recipe candied yams or ambrosia or Waldorf salad— and put out a real groaning board.

In the church or out I have always liked gospel music. My special favorites are Albertina Walker and The Clara Ward Singers and Shirley Caesar and The Caravans. If I could only have one record on a desert island it would have to be "When We All Get to Heaven." Just a coconut tree, that Shirley Caesar record, and me in the spirit.

You know that Weaver has to share his enthusiasm. But sometimes that spirit is not appreciated by others. Back when I was living in Atlanta my Aunt Gloria, she told me, "Dexter, I'm going out of town for the weekend and I want you to keep my boys for me." I said, "OK." I was managing the main Krystal on Peachtree Street at the time, but I was off that weekend. I got together all my gospel LPs—the best stuff like The Mighty Clouds of Joy, Jessy Dixon, and Dorothy Love Coates and the Original Gospel Harmonettes—just the things I knew that the boys would want to hear. I had about twenty of them, and I went over to her house to watch the boys, so excited knowing that Devereaux and Pic and I were gonna have Bible readings and just a good time playing gospel. But just as soon as I'm getting in the door Pic says, "Our record player broke." And I thought, "Oh no, it's broke. Here I got my twenty albums really ready to sanctify them and to have a good time and the hi-fi is broke." Years later Devereaux and Pic told me that all that time whenever they knew Cousin Weaver was coming over to watch them, they would be looking out the window to see if I was toting those albums and if I was, they would run along to the living room and just steal the needle out of that stereo.

I met evangelist Patricia Diggs when she preaching the Word at Pastor Naomi Durant's church, one of the largest Holiness churches in Baltimore in the early seventies. You know how sometimes when you're out evangelizing and the message you are laying down is real, real good, after service somebody will come up and say, "Ooh, I really enjoyed that message. You really enlightened me. Give me your phone number 'cause I'm sponsoring a service to raise money for our building fund and I'd like to get you to come and speak." Well, I heard Evangelist Diggs preach and I told her that I enjoyed her and we exchanged numbers. I started calling her and putting her on platform services and to ministering some night services. She was just very happy for the opportunity.

Evangelist Diggs was medium tall with a light complexion and the prettiest salt and pepper hair. She had eight children and she worked as a private duty nurse. Evangelist Diggs always believed in hard work, like me, and she always kept a nice house.

She and I were very close, she taught me a lot in that ministry in Baltimore. Evangelist Diggs and I would travel around to various churches and she preached the real strong gospel. She didn't dilute it. She did the whole truth and nothing but the truth, you know, whether anyone liked it or not. Her job was to do the work of evangelism and people would be delivered through her.

She was made of fire and brimstone for sure. One thing Sister Diggs used to say was "when me and my husband was out in the world at the cabarets, we'd be the first ones on the dance floor and the last ones off." So when she left the sinful world to start working for the Lord, she was always the first one on the floor praising God and the last one to stop the yelling.

Because she was Sanctified she preached a lot about that baptism and told the people that if they ever wanted to see Him they'd better get baptized in His name. And they'd better really feel that baptism, become a new creature as the water washed away their sin and worldly desires. She said, "Lot of people go down a dry devil and come up a wet one."

She followed a "clothesline religion" where the women couldn't wear pants or the short-short skirts and there were so many rules about dating and marriage. And she believed it all, but Evangelist Diggs never thought that as a female she shouldn't be in the pulpit or that it was man's work or anything like that. Of course, some think that leading souls has got to be a man's work because its the most important work there is. But Evangelist Diggs thought that since it is the most important work there is it shouldn't be trusted only to men. Whosoever gets the calling has got to answer it. Maybe women have the natural advantage here. Turn that Bible saying upside down, that "if the head is sick, the body is sick." If mothers can nurture the body, prepare and serve their children their daily meals, maybe they are the best to prepare and serve up the message of the Word. The authority in the church comes from God and if Gods calls a woman to be a bishop, the menfolk had better stand aside.

Sister Diggs knew the best way to get her husband Charles to believe was to let him see the light of the Lord shining from within her, to live as an example to him, thereby winning him. She didn't go home and just condemn her husband. They have a scripture that says that if you're saved then you can sanctify your household. She really emphasized on that a lot in her ministry. If people might not be ready to give up the dope, the cigarettes, the swinging-out fornicating, what can you do but lead by example? God is stronger than all those things and if you let His presence be felt in the room *through you* then that doper, that smoker, that sexed-up one will feel God through you and will want to plug into the power. You be the socket! I used to use this term in my own ministry, "You gotta catch a fish 'fore you can scale him." And Sister Viola gave me the correction, "Not only that, brother, but you first got to bait your hook." So this friend of mine, Gwen, she corrected Viola. She said, "But even before that, sister, you got to have a mind to go fishing."

One time Evangelist Diggs had a vision of neon lights flashing "money, money, money." She interpreted that to relate to the signs that hang over church fronts. Some signs might say "saint" or "holy" or "mission," but really they're all about "money, money, money." That's all some churches are concerned with, and she wanted to get souls delivered from that. She was not interested in getting a big offering or anything. She cried out against all of these anniversaries and bake sales, stuff that wasn't edifying to the church. In her ministry she was all the time saying, "It's dangerous to play church, y'all."

One of the other things she preached against was witchcraft. She said she knew witchcraft first hand because she saw it when she was growing up and she saw it in the community and the church. She said, "I grew up in it, I was raised in it, I married in it, and I'm still in it." That was one of her testimonies.

Well, I know the average person if their luck is down or something they'll say, "I believe my girlfriend working roots on me." A lot of people here, if they're having any type of disturbance or confusion among the brethren or any kind of downfalls or if their man or woman quits them they might feel as though somebody is working root against them. It could mean that their enemy is actually going in the ground and getting the plants that only the root doctors know, grinding them up, and casting the powder over them or injecting it into their food. Or it could mean that somebody is casting some old hoodoo-voodoo-type spell, divining bad luck and hardship to come their way. Doing things to their photo—drawing on it or talking against it or burying it in pieces. Sometimes even church folk will talk this way. And I know a lot of folk facing time in jail say they will go to see a lady here in Athens and she'll tell 'em that when they go into the courtroom they should take this little bottle of root ground-up and just let it sprinkle out of their sleeve onto the floor. The judge won't see it, just that little bottle of stuff, but that root will work a spell and the lady tells 'em, "If you do that, you'll get off scot-free."

Evangelist Diggs and I ministered at a church one night, I don't think I should flat-out mention where it's located, and some of the people were telling Evangelist Diggs that the pastor would "see people," you know how some of these pastors *see* folk in private, giving them numbers and telling them if they do this, that, and the other they will have luck. A lot of pastors give out numbers and tell folk to get a rabbit foot and all this kind of mess. So Evangelist Diggs began to cry out against all the witchcraft that is in the church as well as in the world.

I had some workers, Felicia, who was still in the twelfth grade, and Damien, who'd just got out of high school. Damien liked Felicia, and Damien's girlfriend, she disliked Felicia 'cause she thought Damien was trying to get with Felicia. Felicia had a cold or something one night. So Felicia, me and her went to the Winn-Dixie and she got two or three different medicines for her cold. You know young folks, they'll take two Alka-Seltzer Plus and some Bayer aspirins and two or three more OTCs. Felicia woke up the next morning, her lip was swoll out like this, her eyes were puffed, her hands bloated. She came to me and asked me, "Dexter, you think Damien's girlfriend working root on me?" And I said "Aww, girl, you worse than your mother." All her mother talked about is roots. These people have all been raised in witchcraft and spells and they don't realize that the simple explanation is the best, that their problems come from inside them, things that they could get a handle on themselves if they'd just try. If you're broke, it's probably because you're trifling, and if your girlfriend quit you, it might be because you're low down. No need to give Dionne Warwick's psychic friends $3.99 a minute to break it down for you. Some folks will never say, "I'm reaping what I sowed." They're all the time wanting to say, "I can't get no job, I'm about to be put out, everything I touch turns to shit. Somebody must be working root on me."

People do this all over. My grandmother Rena laid it all out for us two Labor Days ago. I have a Labor Day function over here every year. (You know Weaver is all about labor so Labor Day would have to be my deal.) So for my labor function I have a big cookout in the yard. All my aunts and cousins come in from Atlanta and everywhere. I guess we have about fifty or sixty Weavers, Bradleys, and whoever else wants to party. I bring the picnic tables from in front of the restaurant; it's always a big, big function. And my grandmother was out there talking that year.

She said, "Look out for those rooty folk. Them folk from Oglethorpe is *real* rooty. Don't trust nobody from Oglethorpe County and don't trust nobody from North Carolina either, 'cause they are just as rooty, maybe worse."

My dad's girlfriend, Miss Evelyn, was out there. Miss Evelyn was born in North Carolina and lived in Oglethorpe County, Georgia.

So she said, "Miss Rena, I was born in North Carolina and now I live in Oglethorpe County."

I remember Grandmama said, "Honey, I don't mean no harm, but they just like that there. They just are."

And Miss Evelyn, she was laughing so much she was crying, and the only thing she could get out was, "They *are* rooty, Miss Rena. In truth they *are*."

But I don't go by all that old witchy mess. I'm about like Bishop Solomon who said, "I got a root that'll work where yours won't. You have to work up a spell, but all I have to do is ask."

Evangelist Diggs had this remarkable ability to walk into a church and remark on what was covered up in that congregation. You know, these folk are all for the money, these other folk are doing root work, this here church needs to be released from sin. Almost like a diagnosis. Whatever was covered up, when you got her to come in and do you a revival, she'd uncover it. Automatic. When she got to the church, she really praised the Lord, got right into the service. With a ministry of condemnation and repentance and remission of sin, many times you don't have a lot of disciples. So you can figure out that Evangelist Diggs didn't have many followers, but she did have some. She had me and she had a good prayer partner, Sister Delores, who was also ministering.

One time Sister Diggs went to a revival in North Carolina and she told me later that she had had that place tore up from the floor up. Hammering away at all the things that set her off. After the second day of the revival Evangelist Diggs went outside and saw that her car had four flat tires. I can just see her, starting in right there in the parking lot praising the Lord for her flat tires. "The devil is in that church and he's hearing the Word. He knows I got him cornered and he's convinced a wicked sinner to come out and fight me." Evangelist Diggs thought that getting vandalism committed against her was a victory, a *victory*. She said that for the cause of Christ, she'd be willing to die, so what was a couple of flat whitewalls to her?

Sister Diggs was diagnosed with cancer of the breast in 1980. She received that bad news from her doctors just like she gave the Good News from the Bible: with dignity and forbearance. I went to see her in the Diggs's apartment on Sutton Place in Baltimore thinking I was gonna have to encourage her, but Lord, she still was ministering from her sickbed and giving *me* encouragement. She knew all the different stories of Job, how he was sick so long the flesh fell off his bones and how he cursed the day of his birth. She knew all about that, so she was still rejoicing, still believing in God, knowing that everybody has got to be somewhere, so if she's absent from the body here, she's present with the Lord over there. Sister Diggs went on home to Jesus Christ in 1985, beat up but not beaten.

Now let me explain something to you that might be hard for you to understand if you are not Holiness Church, and that is that Sister Diggs's funeral was a joyous, joyous event. Ooh, Lord. The Bible says cry for those who are coming into the world, and rejoice for those who are going out. So that's what we do.

Let me tell you how we went to Sister Diggs's funeral. Sister Viola, she always likes to be included, she and Sister Bell and I all piled in my Monte Carlo in Athens bound for Baltimore. And Sister Viola said, "We gonna pray before we take off to Baltimore," and we all prayed a good long prayer and then we started up the road. Looks to me like in South Carolina, in the middle there, a little snow started spitting. We got all the way to North Carolina, the snow getting worse every mile. And it just stayed constant all up through North Carolina, all through Virginia, all through D.C., all through Baltimore. My Monte was in real good shape when we left Athens. But in route, all the systems went *ker-fuffle* one by one; let me click them off for you—rear defroster broke, gas pan broke, speedometer broke, heat just barely making it. Me and the church ladies barreling through a snowstorm in my Monte Carlo coming apart at the seams, singing hymns and putting cold pedal to the metal to get to Evangelist Diggs's funeral. Imagine that.

I don't believe that Sister Diggs had a wake. Depending on if the family wants one, a wake might come before a Holiness funeral. The wake would probably be held the day before the funeral and at the same church where the body is laid out. If there is a wake, it'll probably wind up being a service in and of itself, 'cause a choir will sing or somebody will give a solo, and then the spirit might start working around the room.

But up North they do it different, if I'm not mistaken. I went up to Philadelphia to my aunt's funeral there. That was the first time I had ever been to a night funeral. They have night funerals up North, like in Philadelphia, Baltimore, places all like that. And then they bury you that next morning about eight or nine o'clock. You have a wake and everything, but its all at night. Everybody gets dressed up at night to go to the funeral. Then they go back tomorrow morning for the burial.

After all the snow and cold and breakdowns on the way to Baltimore, when we got there that funeral was filled with warmth, that funeral was spirit-driven and rejoicing. Hey, there's prayer sister Dolores still going around praying to God with a full voice. All the saints say "Hallelujah!"

On the way up from Athens, Sister Viola wouldn't tell me or Sister Bell what she was going to sing, and she has so many favorites I couldn't figure it out on the whole drive up, and that's a twelve- to fourteen-hour drive. Sister Viola got up on that microphone and sung, "When you hear of my homegoing, don't worry about me, I'm just another soldier going on home." And, Lord, those drums and everything were going and everybody was praising God. "When you hear I done left here and went on, don't worry about me." And we had a sure 'nough rejoicing that night. See that's the way Evangelist Diggs lived, you know, and that's the way she died. We were to rejoice and celebrate the living. At a Holiness funeral a lot of times I've heard the minister say, "I'm not here to preach to the dead. They have lived they life. The dearly departed was filled with the Holy Ghost, she accepted the Lord, she told others about the Lord. My

At the beginning of my evangelism days. I still have that old Bible.

job is to speak to the living." And they'd go on and deal with the ones that's there.

Like Evangelist Diggs, William Patterson inspired me in my evangelism. When we met in 1970, Brother Patterson was a reverend at St. Martin's Church of Christ in Baltimore. Because I was just a little more than a child myself, the first thing I noticed about him was his childlike spirit. He was a tall man, but he even had freckles, just like a child. The Bible speaks about us having to have a childlike spirit in order to learn and to be taught, but I think you have to have the same wonder in order to be a teacher too. Brother Patterson had that and when he went into a congregation they always got that same wonder and freshness from him, like he had just discovered the truth that he was speaking. You must come as a child. Jesus spoke about that.

Right after we met, Brother Patterson decided he wanted to add a music ministry to his preaching so he formed the William Patterson Singers and asked me to join. He led the group in singing and I sang tenor and bass and two church ladies named Doris and Diane were the other voices. We'd perform throughout Baltimore, a lot of little programs, and at Annapolis, Maryland. He had that child's go-go-go spirit so he'd always be thinking of new places for us to perform and share the spirit.

I had never sung from the pulpit before and to this day I don't really feel as though I have a singing voice. But back then when I really had someone to lead me in the key I could do a passable tune. All things are possible in Jesus, even getting me to hit a right note. One night at this Holiness church we were singing, "God's not dead, He's still alive. He's just like fire shot up in my bones," and the organ and the drums and everything kicked in, *ooh*, it was so beautiful. The Lord really used me with that song. When I went back to that same church later on, somebody tapped me on the back and asked me, "Could you please sing 'God's not dead, He's still alive'?" That was my first request so I sang it right there and then.

In addition to singing with the William Patterson Singers, I also went out to sing and preach with Mother Johnson. Me and Mother Johnson had met, remember, back in my days at Mergenthaler Vo-Tech because I was friends with her daughter Phyllis. I liked all those Johnsons. They were good people. People persons. They also were short. Mother Johnson was 4' 11", I believe she said she was. Her husband was short. Phyllis was short. All the sisters were short. They had a short brother. All the grandchildren were short. And me and Mother Johnson, we would go out evangelizing and ministering together.

At the time, around 1975, I had a red Volkswagen Beetle. Candy-apple red. Four speed. It had had a couple of little wings and dings in the back so I had to keep it shut with a wire coat hanger wrapped from the trunk handle to the bumper. For real. It burned a little oil, too, but it always started and always finished getting you where you wanted to go. When I was taking nutrition classes at Baltimore Community College there weren't many students who owned their own cars, so for a couple of dollars I would run folks here and there. I was what you might call a hack or a hacker, a gypsy cabbie. My friend Elaine Simon ran a beauty shop out of her kitchen, doing straightening and coloring and all that. And the weaves. Do not forget the weaves. For a while, I was almost the official hack of that beauty shop. At first I just took the ladies home after their hairdo was done, but when everybody stopped being shy, they'd call me before their appointment and I would roundtrip them. I had so many people, and so many big people, in that passenger seat, that pretty soon it started breaking down, looking real low and slung back, like a Barcolounger on the recline. Every time I'd swing around a sharp corner on those little Baltimore alleys, those broke-down springs would spring forward and almost throw my passenger out. From recliner to ejector seat in nothing flat. Elaine called it "The Go-Anywhere, Do-Anything Beetle." (I want you to know that Elaine Simon got her degree and she is now Dr. Simon and she is chief inspector of the beauty salons in Baltimore. Her own salon is called A Touch of Paris Coiffures.) On Sundays I would go pick up Mother Johnson and we would just have a glorious time, Mother Johnson prophesying and speaking in tongues and just having a good time. If she felt she had to, she'd just start speaking in tongues right there in The Go-Anywhere, Do-Anything Beetle.

Speaking in tongues is like the evidence of the Holy Ghost. Paul talked about the gift of tongues in 1 Corinthians 12:1 and 10. God gives it as a gift, but only to some, those that are water-baptised, and He does it so that the speaker can self-edify. Yes, I've spoken in tongues myself. It feels real good, the whole thing. Time goes on but you are just caught up in the spirit, and time just doesn't have any meaning, and you couldn't hold a bad thought in your head if you tried. There's a minister who said, "If we were all filled with the Holy Ghost then the jails would be up for rent." You might start jumping on one foot, or waving your arms, or fall down on the floor and start rolling around. That's why, years ago, they used to call some speakers Holy Rollers. There are ushers or nurses in the churches who keep tabs on all the people who fall out and start speaking in tongues. I've been in churches where the ladies fall on the floor and their dresses will go up, and the nurses keep little pieces of fabric they wrap around the ladies to keep 'em from exposing theirselves. But you can't hurt yourself if you are really in the spirit. You might knock yourself in the head or hit your shinbone on the pew, but you won't feel it, the power of the Lord is filling you so strongly there is no room for pain or hurting or anything except for that white light.

Later, me and Mother Johnson and Phyllis and all of 'em became so close we organized a gospel group called the Johnson Singers which included all her grandchildren.

Dorothy Norwood had this song, "Some people think they'll always be around. Some people think they'll never be down." Something about you should go to the mirror and take a look at yourself. It was a real big hit and the Johnson Singers sang this song at various church anniversaries. I was taller than the rest of the singers, those Johnsons are all short, remember, so I would direct them while down on my knees.

Once somebody told Mother Johnson, "You call them the Johnson Singers, but none of them go by the name of Johnson." That's 'cause the group was mostly girls, and I guess they took their husbands' or fathers' last names. But we sang at the churches throughout Baltimore and me and Mother Johnson would go around from church to church on our own also.

Mother Johnson could see all the gifts of the spirit in me 'cause she is like a prophet. She has always prophesied on me and told me I would be very useful to the Lord. She would be going on in tongues and everything. And she said, "Ooh, all the gifts, the Lord is just using you and you are magnifying Him." When I left Baltimore in 1978 to head down here to Georgia, Mother Johnson did the sweetest thing. She organized a farewell program for me and Barbara Ceasar sang and the Johnson Singers did a song, and so did many other groups and choirs. We had Prophet Mills there and Elder Barber, and, *ooh*, the program was so great I almost didn't want to leave Baltimore.

When I did my own ministering without Evangelist Diggs or Pastor Patterson or Mother Johnson, I did all kinds of church work: youth evangelism, MC-ing a lot of programs for anniversary and building fund events and such. At the height of my evangelism I would go to three or four churches a Sunday praising the Lord. My greatest song was "Lift Him Up." I always sang that before I preached. I was my own opening act, you could say.

The way I really got started preaching is through the testimony service. Sometime in the morning before the regular morning service, Holiness Churches will have about fifteen-twenty minutes of testimony service. A testimony service is like a service that all the people in the church can take a part in. You can sing a song, testify, thank the Lord for this, that, and the other, and everybody takes a part. A lot of Holiness churches mostly have it in the morning before the regular service, and then you go on into the morning service with your vessel ready to receive, already with the fire burning. Its sort of like a warm-up act, too.

My favorite kind of program to preach though, besides the jubilee service which is mostly singing and only a little preaching, was the platform service. That's where all different ministers get up and speak on different subjects. That way you get to see one Bible teaching broken down from many different ways and you can study it from a variety of angles. I was in Washington, D.C., in 1982 at a Youth for Christ convention at Way of the Cross Church, and I was one of the evangelists on the platform. The centerpiece of the afternoon, before the Chain Prayer and the Banner Raising, was our 7UP service. We had elders, ministers, and evangelists all preaching on somesuch to UP-lift the people: WAKE UP!, GET UP!, STAND UP!, LOOK UP!, CLEAN UP!, PRAY UP!, HOLD UP! My remarks were on LOOK UP!: "Look up, for your redemption draws nigh." Now that revived the spirit. Those type of conventions also make you merry with food and music and music and food. Also, all the brothers and sisters wear their color-coded name badges: yellow if they're single, white if they're married. That way they know who they should be fellow-shipping with at Social Time right from the get-go.

Travelling around to all those churches I saw so many folk who are set in their ways, stingy in their hearts, not being moved by the Spirit. And that transfers over to their life in the world as well. Those same folk are set in their jobs, stingy with money, not moving up. They are in a kind of waking coma. Back in my ministering days and in my work with people today, I try to get folk to live fully, in the spirit and in the world. Brothers and sisters, *come out of that coma!*

YOU GOT TO RELEASE!

◆ 7 ◆

No matter what, just keep on
with the keep-on.
Automatic.

◆WITH lots of jobs behind me, my vo-tech degree in my back pocket, and filled with the Holy Spirit, the professional Weaver was ready to get on his way. I'd always wanted to go back down South. I had all those good memories of summers there hanging with Robert Lee and the Weavers and eating Grandmama Frances's good cooking. Now was just the right time, I was thinking. My car was mint then, a '78 Monte Carlo with the new-style bucket seats, silver grey. Yes, all my big material needs were taken care of. So one day around Christmas of '78, I just hopped in the car and said, "I'm goin' by faith, goin' home to Athens." Well, it didn't happen exactly that way. You know I resigned from my job as a mail clerk at the Baltimore City Hospital and I did it the right way, gave my two-week notice.

When I was leaving the North, my mother and my cousins and everybody said, "You going back down there to low pay and hard times in Georgia?" I stepped out with three car payments in my pocket knowing by faith I would come here and possess the land.

Part of the reason I wanted to go South was that I had had a dream that I was going to move down to Athens and work with a church. A church like so many I had seen through my evangelism, that had just a few old-timers with hard spirits, and I would take that church and rebuild it. And I felt it perfect in my heart that I could just come in with a brand new vision, have bake sales and rummage sales, get together people to work and draw the young people with my evangelistic ministry. I did find and work with a downtrodden Sanctified church and I worked very hard and I put on the yard sales and I put on the bake sales and I ministered and I worked with young people and all. There were many yokes to be broken because they were set old in tradition and things like that. Still, I made a little progress. We really raised money, we attracted a few young people. And I even had a concert. Some friends of mine out of Baltimore, they used to sing with Clara Ward. Calvin Statham and his wife

Madeline were Clara Ward singers, you know. I invited them down from Baltimore, and we had a pig picking, a big dinner, and raised money for the building fund for the church. We had raffle tickets and we fed the singers. They enjoyed coming because everybody from the North really wants to come to the South 'cause they know one thing about us is that we really lay the food out. They wanted to feel that Southern hospitality they don't get up North.

Just about the time I set foot in Atlanta, I went to a family funeral where I got a lesson that has changed my life. And the lesson didn't come from the pulpit or from any of the friends who gave remarks over the body. It came from a total stranger, but it changed me just the same as if it had been a fire and brimstone sermon or a heavy parable.

I was riding in the procession out to the graveside and I shared the back of a car with some friends of the family and a lady I had never laid eyes on. All of us were just about torn up, but this little lady, don't ask me her name because I didn't even catch it at the time, had a dry eye and a look on her face as calm as any you'd see on a marble statue in a museum. We were talking about different things, just trying to make that long ride pass. But you know how people are, when they should be trying to uplift themselves and concentrate on the positive, they will focus on the negative as sure as shooting. So we were just listing all the tragedies the family had shared and all the sadness we'd seen them through. And this little lady sat there and listened to those downfalls and pitfalls listed one by one and didn't speak a word, until at last she turned to me and said, "Honey, I have done given all that burden to the Lord. Now is the time that you have to *release!*"

She was a saved lady and she went on to tell us how she believed that one day when she died she would release to the Lord her very soul, her eternal spirit, and that she wanted to know in her bones that that was true and she wanted to send up her spirit to the Lord all joyful. Giving up her soul to Him was such an act of faith that while she was still alive she knew she would have to get in the habit of releasing all the things of life, the heartaches from kids, disappointments from her husband, worries about bills, so she could see that the Lord would take care of them one way or another. Seeing the Lord receive her daily burdens would let her know that He would one day receive her soul.

When I got out of the car after talking to that little saved lady I felt as light as a bird. I released it in that car! I wanted to yell out at the graveside, "Get on up there, friend, you've been released!"

Now I'm releasing everything. Employee problems, sickness, strife in the world, I am giving them all to the Lord. That doesn't mean that I don't try to fix things that are broken or that I just roll over and accept everything. It means that I'm like Paul from the Bible, I'm forgetting those things which are behind me, and I'm reaching for those things which are before me.

I want to give you an example of the way your life moves when you learn to release. You know that Go-Anywhere, Do-Anything Beetle I had back in Baltimore before I got my Monte Carlo? Candy-apple red, remember? There's something I didn't tell you.

Mother and me were the first black family to move onto Madison Street near Highlandtown. Some of our neighbors there, one family in particular, wanted us to know that we weren't welcome. There were a couple of boys in that neighbor-family who took their baseball bats and keys and hammers and such and just trashed that Go-Anywhere, Do-Anything Beetle until it was so beat up it looked like it had been stalled on the railroad tracks. Of course, I could have hated those boys and carried that burden around with me forever. But how could Weaver have gone anywhere or done anything with a 2,000-pound Beetle on his back? For real. Without knowing what to call it, I released it. I released the burden, the hate, the anger, all that mess, and went on. Back on the bus route. So that's why I just slipped in that silver grey Monte Carlo to you.

You should try this, to release your trouble. Start small. Some of those big things that tested Job, you might have to work yourself up to those. But start to release the small things that trouble you and see what happens in your life.

Around the end of March of '78 I started with Kentucky Fried Chicken. So I stayed on in Athens, working in KFC management and with St. John's Holiness Church, until about 1980 when I moved to Atlanta.

And there I was hired as assistant manager at Krystal. I went through job training at the Krystal on Fulton Industrial, it was the training store, and then the area manager took me to my store down on Peachtree Street. There

on Peachtree Street was what might be called the red-light district. And me as an evangelist had been sort of sheltered. I guess they called it red-light because the light of day never shines on half the stuff that went down on midtown Peachtree Street in the seventies. For real.

In Atlanta, at twenty-seven, I bought my first house. The bank man took me to the house and it had been redone, floors, walls, everything, and it was just beautiful. It was a rancher-style house, half red

I didn't have so much money, so I traveled by faith to Atlanta in my '78 Monte Carlo. I loved that Monte. This photo was taken at my house on Larkspur Drive in Atlanta.

brick and half white wood. It had a good-sized carport for my Monte. So I applied, I guess me and three or four other people, and out of all of them, I got it. I had real good credit, especially for a young person. And I was just real happy about it, the first house I could remember anyone in our family owning for a long time.

Along about this time I met and married Maxine Underwood. I loved her a lot but in the end our religions kind of crossed. Maxine was saved and in Holiness too, but I was more in the strict Holiness, as you know from before. She felt like I was too possessed by the material things. She would say I cared too much about my house and my car, "You worship these bricks and mortar. You worship this tin and paint." But I never felt like I did that. I'm not the sort of person to be jumping out there washing his van in twenty-degree weather trying to keep the shine on it. Well, it took us about six months to know that we'd always be a little further apart than we would be together, so we decided to go on our separate paths.

Since I've always kept my eyes on Him, I've always been looking up. So even if I couldn't work it out with Maxine, I wanted to keep on with the keep-on. I had my house, so now I wanted to get to work on building the rest of my future.

When I first went to Baltimore with my mother in 1962, Robert Lee introduced us to his sister Fanny Maude and her husband Jerome Mosby. Looks like to me in Georgia, everyone has lots of middle names, like Robert Lee had a sister named Marion Jane—she saw visions of my success—and people call my mother Carrie Emily—if they've known her a while they might swirl it around some kind of way and it will come out "Caremma." Sometimes when folk leave the South, they drop their middle names at the bus depot.

Mother paid Fanny Maud maybe twenty-five dollars a week for her and Robert Lee to stay there and Mother said she bought groceries and she helped cook on Sunday. I was still down South with Bo and his wife Magnolia. When Mother got herself established she came down to get me. And that's when little Weaver became acquainted with Mr. Jerome and Fanny Maud his own self.

The Mosbys were always an inspiration for everyone around here in a lot of different ways. Remember that back when those two moved up North that was the time that most black folks around this part of the South were doing day work, cleaning houses, working in the chicken-plucking factories, and all like that. But when Mr. Jerome and Fanny Maud went to Baltimore they sort of set up home base for the family. And soon the Eberharts were drifting up North to get theirs just like Mr. Jerome and Fanny Maud had done.

When I was young and fresh from the country, Mr. Jerome sort of took me under his wing. I really took to him too. Even at a young age I felt I was a leader and I saw that Mr. Jerome was a leader too. Mr. Jerome was slow to speak but quick to smile, his words were wise and his smile was infectious. There was that straight-off connection.

The last day of school before fall break I would catch that Baltimore Transit bus and go out to the Mosbys's house to help Fanny Maud get the Thanksgiving ready. I thought I was something going out to Mr. Jerome's house. On the bus all the way to Gwynn Oak Park. Those houses sitting by theirselves with all those rooms. The Mosbys had a big front porch and a big back porch and they had a basement and an upstairs, you know. And even though everybody was coming, Mr. Jerome and Fanny Maud had enough room to hold them all.

My job was to help clean the greens. You know, help pick through 'em and wash the grit off 'em. Sometimes she might do turnip greens, and you know, turnip green leaves are smaller than the big collards so, *ooh*, trying to go through five or ten pounds of them will really take a long time. And then they would also do chitlins. Robert Lee and all of them cleaning 'em and then cooking 'em with hog maws to stretch 'em. I learned how to do chitlins watching Mr. Jerome and Robert Lee. To this day, before any family get-together they all say, "Dexter, we want you to do the chitlins." And, boy, that's one of the first things to go, those chitlins. You set the pot down on the Weaver table and by the time you turn around twice, when you go fishing around in there with a spoon you won't pull up nothing but juice. Every last chitlin will be *gone*. So each year we about have to increase the amount. Even if you you do fifty pounds this Thanksgiving you'll be thinking maybe I should do a little more at Christmas.

For big family get-togethers, Thanksgiving and Christmas and funerals, all roads back then led to Mr. Jerome's and

Fanny Maud's house. Even though we went to the Mosbys's for those holidays, the rest of the family still cooked up a storm, making all that good food from back home, all the Georgia delicacies. Fanny Maud and them, even though they was in the North, they still had all their Southern ways and they wanted their Southern supper. She'd put on a pot of pig feet and pig ears in a minute. She'd also get some bunches of collards and put them in a pot, I'm talking about a big old huge pot, oversized almost like a restaurant pot. Fanny Maud also made the best walnut cake. That cake was always tall. Maybe a four layer. You could turn it this way and that way and it would still be too big for your jaw, like trying to get a sideways ladder through a lengthwise door.

Everybody else brought covered dishes. Whatever they were famous for they'd make, just three or four times the amount, and put it in their best dish and wrap it up in Saran Wrap and kitchen towels, so much padding you'd think they were transporting dynamite. Now if you want to take a break here and look around the back of the book at some of those recipes, go on. Don't they look *good*?

Of course, we had the Christmas music. Oh yeah, an R&B Christmas. The Tempts's *Give Love at Christmas* album on Motown . . . and "Bells will be ringing" . . . "Please Come Home for Christmas" by Charles Brown. And I loved "Gee Whiz, It's Christmas" by Carla Thomas. You remember Carla and Rufus Thomas did some songs together, they were real big in the sixties and seventies. Rufus had a lot of nicknames:

The Crown Prince of Dance, The World's Oldest Teenager, and The Funkiest Man Alive. And they always played that "Gee Whiz, It's Christmas" on the radio every year. And then Patti LaBelle and The Bluebelles with their "What Are You Doing New Year's Eve?" Patti says "it's much too early in the game, but what are you doing on New Year's Eve?"

But we'd get all the holiday meal prepared. The turkey and ham and all the good greens and pies. A groaning board of everything you'd want to eat. And the people just came and came. It seemed like everyone who ever called themself a Mosby or an Eberhart was in that house. And, ooh, the drinks would really be going flowing. One thing about Mr. Jerome was, shoot, every time he went down to his cellar and came back up, he'd be opening up a fifth of this, a fifth of that. They were loving that Johnny Walker Red and the corn liquor. They had themselves a good old time.

But Mr. Jerome was a different kind of drinker, not like those kind I'd seen going back and forth in front of my shoeshine stand, those who drank 'til their stomachs were full and their wallets were empty. Mr. Jerome just wanted everybody to have some fun, to lubricate the wheels, you might could say, to see his house as the place to be. I guess today we'd call it responsible drinking.

Mr. Jerome just had a business mind. To my knowledge I don't think Mr. Jerome really had a lot of formal education. He might could read a little bit and write a little bit, but I

don't think he's one that finished high school or went on to
college. But if you are talking about doing the most with
what you have, then that was Mr. Jerome. He was all the
time with his ear to the ground, listening for a good deal or
a bargain. And I'm not saying the things he got were hot or
anything like that, what you would say *stolen*. He wasn't
about that, it was just that he knew what was on the market,
cars, houses, and whatnot, and he knew how much they were
worth and what they should cost. Mr. Jerome and Fanny
Maud also had a place in Lynchburg, Virginia, that's where
Mr. Jerome was from, and they had a place there that they
collected rent off of. Fanny Maud and him also had land here
in Athens on Field Street, land Fanny Maud's mother left her
children, and Mr. Jerome put a trailer on there and started
renting that out. See that business mind he had?

Mr. Jerome would buy all the meat for the family from
places along Corned Beef Row or from a kosher slaughter-
house in Jonestown, not because they were kosher, but just
because it was cheaper than in the stores. The Mosbys and
Mother and Robert Lee would go down every Sunday
morning to Lombard Street to that good bakery that sold
donuts real cheap. I would go with them and we would eat
those warm sugary donuts right on the street with hot coffee. Mr. Jerome would go on and get the greens for their
Sunday supper from the street market or get a roast from
Elberth's Quality Meats in Highlandtown or from Joe's Cut
Rate Meats on Fleet Street in Fells Point. They would get

chitlins (sometimes the already cleaned kind) and fresh eggs and fresh-killed chickens too. Not only was it a good way to s-t-r-e-t-c-h the dollar, but I think it also reminded them of back home where you always got that stuff fresh, instead of flash-froze, freeze-dried, and shrink-wrapped at a supermarket.

Mr. Jerome always had a plan—to help Robert Lee buy his handicap van, to buy this house or that lot of land for the cost of the back taxes, to rent out a property—to get a little more out of life. Thinking ahead, trying to make his own future, making life better for himself and the people he cared about, this might have been the first time I had really seen a body do this. It just came as a revelation to me. In those days I guess we didn't say the word "mentor" but that's what he was to me.

When Mr. Jerome died in 1989 at age seventy-seven I went to his funeral up in Baltimore. Even though by then I was an adult, almost thirty-four years old, I always called him Mr. Jerome, but all the others who'd known him as children, they called him Uncle Jerome. By Mr. Jerome not going to church, when he died they had his service at a funeral parlor. The undertaker got up to ask would anyone like to say any words about Jerome Mosby. And you know, I don't believe a single person got up to give remarks. They left the floor open for fifteen minutes for someone to walk up and say something. You know how somebody dies and somebody else on their job might come to the funeral home and say, "Oh, he was a good person. He believed in doing right. He was always on time. He got along with everybody." No one got up to say anything about Mr. Jerome. And its not that nobody didn't like Mr. Jerome—no, because everyone liked Mr. Jerome, he was well-liked, *well*-liked. Maybe it was just that all our feelings ran too deep to put in a nutshell. There was so much I could, we all could, have said about Mr. Jerome. And I often think today, that I should have been that one . . .

A large part of my later thinking I could make a go of it in my own business came from seeing Mr. Jerome wheel and deal and make those little deals add up to big ones. I think Mr. Jerome lived long enough to see that something was going to come together for me and that he had schooled the business Weaver. I hope it and I think it.

After going back from Atlanta to Baltimore for a little while, I came down to Athens in 1984. I had this brand new car and all these three-piece suits from going to church all the time and singing in choirs and such, so I was just really prepared for a good job. I went to a couple of the fast food places to talk about a job and on the application it asked "salary desired." So there I was with a new car, another silver grey Monte Carlo, and these three-piece suits. And I put down . . . I think minimum wage was then $2.90 and I put down five dollars an hour, you know, 'cause I thought that I should be a supervisor. And a lot of those places, would you know, they practically escorted me to the door by the hand. They were like, "Who do you think you are coming from up North asking for five dollars per hour?" I looked around for a long time, maybe three months or more, with not a whit of luck. I just didn't know what to do.

Then I got to thinking that maybe I didn't look to these folks like I needed a job. Maybe my suits and my new Monte were hindering me out of a job. At that time, my dad had this old 1966 Buick and I thought I'd ride that to look for a job. I had set up an interview at the ATΩ house at the University of Georgia to cook the boys' weekday dinners. I drove my dad's Buick and, just to be sure, I parked her around the corner. I had got the knack then. They gave me the job. I worked five days a week cooking dinner for all the boys who lived in the big frat house on River Road. I got to bring food home and in those first few lean months that came in handy.

Several months later I got a second job catering dinner every night to another frat whose clubhouse was on Milledge Avenue. Every night I would pull up in the junker van I'd bought from my uncle, Tom Lay, and drop off the meat-and-threes for about fifty of the boys.

One day after I'd been catering their meals for a few months I pulled up like I always did at five o'clock and blew the horn for one of the pledges on kitchen duty to come and get it. But that day I was in a brand-new van I'd saved up and bought with money from all my jobs. The next thing I knew one of those boys says, "So, this is where our money is going." And there I'm thinking I'm just getting a new vehicle to serve folk better and there they are nosing around in my business. After all, my uncle's van was an old beat-up ice cream van. The floor so rusted out you could see the center line whiz by as you were driving. What would I look like riding in a van that's broke down, all my tires maybe going to pop, and all this exhausting smoke? Like this girl I know, she was saying her car is backfiring all the time. And when she rides in a rough 'hood with her junker going "pow, pow, pow!", all the people duck down in the streets, thinking she's committing a drive-by. Anyway that boy said, "So this is where our money is gone." The next thing I knew, the very next day, those boys called me and told me they didn't need me anymore. Dropped D like a hot potato.

I took my van home and put it up under my carport and let it stay there for a month or more until I said to myself, "Shoot, I ain't paying notes on a van I can't ride." And I didn't worry about that fraternity that dropped me, I knew that the beat goes on. And it did. Automatic.

Soon after I got back to Athens, I met somebody who would stay a lifetime friend. Miss Ada and I had met when I got her to help me with my frat dinners. She was already about retirement age when we hooked up.

Miss Ada couldn't read or write but anything you sent her to the Piggly Wiggly store for she could get. If it were something in a can, it would have to have a picture on the can. I would say, "I need a can of green beans from the Piggly Wiggly store, Miss Ada." She'd say, "Okey-dokey." She couldn't shop the scratch-and-dent can sales 'cause sometimes those cans don't have pictures on them.

Me and her were the ones to open up at the Athens Fair together in about '85 or '86. That's when I got my first real sign painted up. To tell you the truth it was nothing but an old tin Coke-Cola sign that somebody gave me and I had painted over.

Miss Ada would come over and sleep in my spare bedroom the night before the fair opened. Put all her little things in a paper sack, her cold cream and toothbrush and high-button nightgown. And those pink curlers. Do not forget the pink curlers. She would come over to my house on Meadow Lane and we would turn on the music and get to work. Chopping and cleaning and boiling and baking. Miss Ada would stick with me for the whole run of that fair. She'd be with me the entire time.

We would open up on Sunday, when they would be setting up the rides and we'd feed all the carnie folk and roustabouts who were putting up the rides and the midway. We made the three squares, plus all kinds of cakes and Rice Krispies treats. Those carnie folk can *eat*. We had peanuts and we had candy bars and chewing gum. They told us we couldn't sell cotton candy and we couldn't sell candy apples. You know, things that the fair already sold. But Miss Ada and I were a real big hit. Weaver D's was the first real food, I mean home-cooked food, that some of those people had had for a long time. Monday they'd be ready to kick off, and Miss Ada and me would be there in full effect.

Miss Ada might not have had much in the way of material things in her life, but she always worked hard, was honest, and was not a complainer. You could do worse than be like Miss Ada.

About that time, I also worked making snacks at the 20 Grand Club. That was the hottest dance club to be at in '80s, where everybody in Athens wanted to work the floor. I was back in the back of the 20 Grand making chicken and fried fish sandwiches. I didn't even have a stove or oven, just a double-burner hot plate. I felt as though I could really have throwed out more food if I'd had a stove, I mean if I could do all that with just a little hot plate, with a stove I would have been dangerous.

One thing that happened at the 20 Grand gave me a scare. This young guy who worked at the club, I don't even know his name, was catering on the side too. He came back to the 20 Grand kitchen and said, "I catered at the Black and White Ball at the Forest Lodge." And he said, "Do you know during that affair I got five more caterings?" And I was just going, "*What?*" And I said to myself, "This boy's a go-getter. He is going to run me out of the catering business." That's what I was saying to myself. I ran to the telephone at the 20 Grand and called my friend Laura Day. I just left my kitchen and called up Laura—it was an emergency!

I asked, "Laura, remember that boy from the 20 Grand that caters around here?" I said, "He told me he did the Black and White Ball. He got five other affairs just from that one. He is going to drive me out of business. We don't have formalwear or silver trays or anything like he has."

Me at twenty-three with Laura Day at my first big catering job. We served two hundred hungry folks.
I was just growing a beard.

Laura asked, "Wait a minute. Wait one damn minute. Is he eatin' and drinkin'?"

"What?"

"I asked is the boy eatin' and drinkin'?"

"Yeah, he's had a few."

"Well then, it ain't shit to him!"

I said, "Laura, why do you say that?"

"He ain't doing nothing but lyin'," she said. "You give those club people something to drink and something to eat, and they automatically start telling lies."

"Laura Day!"

Well, the next week that same boy was coming back. "D, where y'all doin' y'all's cookin' at? Could I use that same kitchen?"

And I reported that to Laura and she said, "I told you! I told you! That boy raising your pressure, 'bout to give you a heart attack. When those club types start eatin' and drinkin' they automatically start lying. You don't have to worry about anything from that one."

I said, "Laura Day, you're goin' off. You are old enough to be my grandmother."

I was getting known around town for delivering meals to beauty shops like Shear Performance, Martha Carol's, Sheats Barber & Beauty, and Carolyn's Success Beauty Salon, and I was catering banquets to the black Greeks at UGA, and making snacks at the 20 Grand, so I started having a few little dinners in my house. A small-like group of people who I mostly knew. Those that came would leave a couple of dollars for the food and the fellowship. I was living mostly by faith at the time and those dollars would help me with my Southern Bell and Georgia Power bills. For real. Those dinners started to get talked up too. When word started to get around by mouth, a DJ from the local radio station said, "Brother, you oughtta put this on the radio. Let us do some ads for you." But I didn't want everybody in Creation trampin' in and out of my house.

I was thinking that another way to make some good money was to start selling concessions and snacks around town. I started doing the roasted peanuts in '84. I bought fifty-pound bags of the best raw goobers I could find from a wholesaler and I roasted them real slow in my oven at home or sometimes at my dad's house on Cone Drive.

Every Friday night, there I'd be sitting on a lot across from the Clarke Central High School football field, sitting out there with my little peanut cart and my little chair. "Peanuts, peanuts! Weaver D peanuts!" My old cousin Jerry Green lived across from the CCHS field. One pitch-black Friday night it got bone chilly up around eight or nine o'clock and I was shivering trying to stay warm. The only heat was the dim little heat from the warming tray. I was just shivering away until I felt my cousin Jerry draping his big Army over-coat around my shoulders. He tugged and hugged that thick wool coat around my shoulders so I'd be warmed. I guess he'd seen me under the glow of the streetlight, hunkered over and trying not to freeze. He was in his late sixties and couldn't walk so well but he somehow made it down that big hill in front of his house. He walked down the hill over to me and draped the warmest coat he had round my shoulders. That light from the streetlamp showed him I was shivering, but also that I was trying to do something for myself and for our name. That kindness of cousin Jerry's made me warm that night and for a long time afterward.

I lived in a nice all-brick house with hardwood floors off the Lexington Road. My landlord was Jim Palace, he owns Palace Marine out on Atlanta Highway with his wife Betty. They charged me just $245 a month, this was 1984, and he never went up on me. Jim and Betty used to order a pound cake from me every once in a while. They saw me really trying to get it together, and they wanted to help me out and give me some business.

I had a garden out back of that house and I grew vegetables. I took pecans off the rental tree to use in my baked goods. Also, I had a little street store out of that house where I sold candy, peanuts, and cold drinks, in between making and delivering dinners and roasting peanuts. Oh, and I also used to do a Weaver D chocolate chip cookie when the peanuts were done roasting and the oven was still warm.

I started going around to convenience stores and filling stations and such, and asking the manager, "Can I place my peanuts in here?" A lot of them had already had my peanuts themselves and so they would say yes just about every time. I got 'em in at a few of the Golden Pantry convenience stores, I think at about eight altogether, and the management sent a memo around to those stores saying that they would start carrying my peanuts and to put 'em right on the counter. So most every store you went in most everywhere, you saw Weaver D's peanuts.

When I asked to put my peanuts in this one place, the man said he wanted a real big percentage out of my peanuts. I mean they were my peanuts and my bags and my staples and my ink on the bag, why should he get more of a profit margin than me? I didn't see *him* roasting no peanuts.

"You need to give me thirty cent and you keep twenty cent," he said.

I just stood firm. "No, you get fifteen and I get thirty-five."

He said, "Well, that's a deal-breaker. Just take 'em on outta here then."

And it sort of crushed my spirit a little bit, but then I went around the corner to the next convenience store and this other man had *two* places. He let me put 'em in both of his stores and at a better rate that I was even asking from the first man. See, when one door closes, the Lord opens up another one. Automatic.

A man in town named Mr. Reese Lester would take things like those good skin-on potato chips and pork rinds and all like that and vend them all over northeast Georgia and he started to take orders for my peanuts. I would work a full day at making catering and delivery meals and then start in at night to roast and bag up those hot peanuts. All week long, every night. Many is the night I fell asleep with my head down on the kitchen table with raw goobers and broken shells and paper bags scattered all around me.

On Sundays I would take them down to Mr. Lester's place and put 'em on his truck and he'd distribute them all over northeast Georgia the next day. People was telling me they'd be coming home from church down in Morgan County, walk into the Golden Pantry and see Weaver D's peanuts clear up there.

And next thing you know a guy told me, he said, "Weaver, it's somebody else doin' peanuts like you." A certain store here in Athens started making almost my exact same peanuts—the same color bag, same red ink on the bag, and with a name real close to mine. The guy said, "If you not careful, you'll pick up a bag of those fake peanuts and you think you holdin' Weaver D's!"

Many times during those years that I was putting together my sidelines, bagging peanuts, working at the fair, catering this and that, and running donation dinners out of my house, I would sit at my kitchen table in the evening and say, "Lord, how was I at three places at one time?" You know, like that song, "My Soul Looks Back in Wonder."

Those jobs were some kind of hard work but I saved every dollar I could. Like Mr. Jerome, I can squeeze a dollar bill until George Washington cries "Uncle!" I saved almost fifty percent of my income during those lean years. That was my decision to save up and build, build, but to tell the truth I think I was working too hard to have the time to spend money. You have to deny yourself when you are a small-business person, deny yourself vacations and trips to the mall. But if you keep in mind that what you are doing is buying your future with your money in the bank, you won't feel denied. If you want to someday be looking at the clouds fluff by through the sun roof of your new Lexus, you're going to have to spend a lot of time looking through the rusted-out floor of your ice cream van. Keep your eye on that straight center line.

DELICIOUS
FINE FOODS
→8←

I called it Weaver D's
Delicious Fine Foods
because I am and it is.

→FINALLY I was able to see that what I had been working toward so long and so hard might come true. Maybe taken one by one my past jobs and all my sideline catering might seem like little jobs, but I never saw it that way. I always saw them as building blocks. And now I was ready to go to the next level. I wanted to open my own place. Call it Weaver D's Delicious Fine Foods, serve the people good food and keep a piece of the pie for my own self.

Selling roasted nuts adds up to more than peanuts. I had saved every little last bit I could lo those many years and I had a little nest egg at Athens First Bank and Trust. Just enough to start looking around for a place to call my own. It didn't take long.

The only big thing about the small town of Athens is the grapevine. There are some folk here with ears so big they can hear you thinking. A bunch of people told me about this or that place that would be perfect for a home-style restaurant, but when I first saw what's now Weaver D's Delicious Fine Foods, I knew that that was it. Automatic. Tucked away at the dead end of Broad Street, it had all the room for forty-some seats, two picture windows, a kitchen, a pantry, and a little office for me and Mother to do the bookkeeping. Mr. Roger Sullivan at the lawn mower repair shop next door introduced me to Ed Mingledorff, the owner. A check and a handshake and it was mine. Automatic and hallelujah!

George Lee Taylor and Junior Howard—he's so big they call him "Tank"—said that they would help me get the old place into shape. There was a lot of training going on in Athens in World War II and I think that this old white cinder block building might have been some kind of Army surplus-type building. Like most of us at forty, it needed to be stripped down, washed around, and dressed up.

I would go to the hardware store first thing in the morning, buy whatever paint or Sheetrock or lumber George Lee and Junior would need for the day, drop it off at the restaurant, and head back home to do my catering and sidelines. With the money I earned that day, I'd head back to Normaltown Hardware the following morning, get more nails or plumbing pipe, drop it off for George Lee and Junior, and do the whole thing over. When I didn't have a catering, I would be down with them hammering and nailing and whatnot.

It was hard to keep my mind on my deliveries and catering on the day that George Lee and Junior said that they'd be through with fixing the place up. So much time and money and such high hopes. You know that group Blood, Sweat, and Tears? Weaver could be an honorary member. It just didn't seem real that little Baltimore Dexter, eating government cheese and living by faith preaching the word, would own his own place of business. A dream come true.

When I pulled up to the front of the restaurant, George Lee and Junior had some kind of way found that painted-up Coke-Cola sign from the Athens Fair days with Miss Ada. It was hanging over the front door, *my* front door, telling everybody in Athens that this is the home of

WEAVER D'S DELICIOUS FINE FOODS
AUTOMATIC FOR THE PEOPLE

I just stood and stared and stared, not half believing that after all the thirty-five-cent shines and catered meals and riding around in an ice cream van that this was mine. Finally, I had to go inside. With the wind whipping up the sawdust and paint fumes out there, I knew my eyes would be running like faucets unless I went inside and got back to work.

You should have been there on May 1, 1986, when I had my Grand Opening. Mayor Coile was there and county council members and people from WXAG radio and my father Bo. Mr. Sullivan from the lawn mower shop had let me take his portable light-up sign out near the road to write out "Weaver D Open May 1." Everybody going back and forth east and west on Broad Street had seen that sign for a couple of weeks. Back then the guardrail was not up by the bridge, so in your car you could really just focus in on that sign. And I had my free advertising on *both* sides of that sign. And lit up at night too.

I had a ribbon-cutting ceremony at the Grand Opening of my restaurant on May 1, 1986.
(l to r) Matthew Ware, Mayor of Athens Lauren Coile, Ed Turner, Marie Green, Edward Miggendorf, and me.

I had a jingle which played on the radio for days and days before the opening. Mother and Miss Payne couldn't make it down from Baltimore for the ribbon-cutting so I called both of them and held the telephone receiver right up to the radio when the jingle came on so they could be part of all the happenings.

I was too busy to remember to keep my first dollar bill to frame. But I don't think that I could have afforded to keep George behind glass for very long anyway. I would have had to take him to the Winn-Dixie store and set him to *work*. Everybody was dying to be the first one in the door that morning. Looks like to me Bernice Ford or either Sarah Merrith was the first customer at that grand Grand Opening. Bernice used to help me in my dad's house sell dinners.

Oooooh, the place was so bright and clean. It was just smelling so good. The food and the paint. That new paint smell says to me, "Let's do business." And even though it's a small room, it just seats a little more than forty, you'd think that there were double-double that many people for all the whooping and laughing and back-slapping. My Holiness friends and everybody was coming in, just so happy; it was like the birth of something. Everybody was just so happy right along with me.

I think we closed at six o'clock that first day. We were open six to six. I don't even think we felt it that first night because we were a little younger, lighter, and real energetic. We didn't have any forecast of sales that we were working towards. We were just trying to serve as many people as we could get through that front door.

And we *were* moving people through the door, but restaurants are expensive things to operate. Just opening up, buying the building supplies, the rent, utility deposits, steam table, refrigerator, I could go on all day, cleaned me out. I got pretty broke pretty soon.

Remember back in the schoolyard in Baltimore kids used to play that game of dirty dozens and signify about somebody's family being broke. Everybody was all in the same boat so it didn't matter. You know, "your mama so poor, she think matched luggage is two shopping bags from the same store." Or "your mama so broke, salt and pepper aren't seasonings, they're dinner" or "your mama so broke, she goes to KFC to lick *other* people's fingers." Now I wasn't that kind of broke but I do remember that we had to take steps to keep up appearances, putting those empty tin cans in the glass-front refrigerator to make it look well-stocked. I ended up staring at those same empty cans for about a full year. And you know we took every day's till to the Piggly Wiggly store to buy just enough food to eke us through the next day's lunch rush. Sometimes I thought my customers should just make their checks payable direct to the Piggly and save me some trouble!

But not everyone was wishing Weaver well. I had a series of break-ins at the restaurant. No matter what I did, it seemed like every day, every other day, I'd go in in the morning and find a window jimmied or a door pried open. I didn't leave the till overnight, so mostly what they got was food. One morning I went in to see that somebody had come in and stolen all the food I'd spent the whole night previous fixing. They jacked my whole catering! After that I told my dad Bo that I was going to sit up all night in the restaurant with a shotgun across my knees. Dad said, "There's already one 'Bo' in the family and that's enough. We don't need a *Rambo*, son." So we just double-triple-deadbolted everything and put in a burglar alarm and soon those banditos got tired of stealing my food. You know that that Laura Day would say she hoped they choked on a stolen chicken bone!

Not everyone wanted to see me succeed, out of jealousy or what I don't know. Some people just can't stand to see anybody get ahead. People are always going to try to bring a brother down.

One day I was at the restaurant dressed up and a guy said, "What you doing all dressed up? You ain't supposed to look like that."

I said, "Well, I'm not gonna *live* in the ghetto and *look* like the ghetto too." So that shut him right on up. He went on and got his food and sit down and ate.

When I've had white people working for me somebody'll come in and say, "I see you're an *equal opportunity* employer." Saying it with a raised eyebrow, like they're accusing me. And I say, "Oh yes," and pretend like I don't know what they mean. One brother flat out told me once, "You liking the wrong people." And I said, "No, I'm liking the right people. I know what side my bread is buttered on. And whosoever

119

butters it fastest and longest and the most reliable is going to have my signature on a paycheck. For real."

And I had learned my lesson from working those caterings and from seeing Mr. Jerome. I didn't take my money and blow it. I kept socking it away so that I could build my business, build by increments. Whenever I got word that such and such a business was selling their stove or getting rid of their chairs, I would offer to buy them and haul them away. That way I ended up owning most of the kitchen and catering equipment I once had to rent. In fact, now I rent out some of my own equipment to folk so that all my equipment does double duty paying for itself.

I still kept up my catering and had a lot of regular customers. I kept up with the Deltas and the AKAs and all the black Greeks. Around about '88 or so, ATΩ hired me to do a big outdoor party. When I went to the house on River Road one of the boys opened the door and out ran a big black dog, snarling and barking. Cujo, I am coming *with* dinner, *I* am not the dinner. I dived onto the nearest car and when I came down onto the windshield of that Maxima, I busted it out. And do you know that I jumped on the right car. It belonged to the owner of the dog, a boy named John Fiveash. John was hot under the collar and told me that he thought I should pay for him a new windshield. My lawyer said, "I don't think you're obligated to pay for that window because looks like to me when you're going over there on business, your safety should be provided without dogs coming out attacking you. Especially at a fraternity house where they're really probably not supposed to have dogs anyway."

And I told Laura Day that this guy was calling me and telling me I'm gonna pay for his window. I told her he said, "Because if you don't pay for it, let me tell you what I'm gonna do. I'm gonna blackball you all over the university. You won't be getting no fraternity and sorority business no more." And I really needed that fraternity business back then. Miss Laura said, "I don't know, D. You might need to pay for it." And that is not the kind of stance that you would expect from Laura Day, so I thought I better go ahead and give John Fiveash a check. Whether or not he would have made good on that threat I don't know, but I guess you catch more flies with honey than you do vinegar, so I put a windshield in that Maxima.

The Bible says do all things without murmuring or complaining. I didn't complain, I didn't bicker, not one iota. I went on and paid for that windshield.

John and I saw eye to eye after that. Because of our dealings I hired him. John was a real good person I came to find out. He treated my business like his own and he was a real hard worker. He would take his dress shirt off, push the sleeves of his long-sleeved T-shirt up to his elbows and wash those dishes, then put all the chairs on the table and mop the floor, just like he held the deed to the place. And me and him one time went all the way out in Oglethorpe County, and this was a sure-enough black area, and he was OK with this. When we were out there catering and we needed something else from the restaurant, I asked, "John, I'm gonna give you the key to the restaurant, you think you can find your way back down in here?" He said, "Oh yeah, I can, D."

He worked for me for about a school term, catering and cashiering and washing dishes. He was a small little fella and a well-mannered child too. He was about business. Not monkey business but money business. Next thing I know John Fiveash was the treasurer of ATΩ fraternity house. He called me and said, "Weaver, we want you to cater dinner for us on a daily basis." And I was able to make a good sum from that fraternity that school term. See what that four hundred dollars could have kept me from?

I stayed so busy at Weaver D's that I'd usually come home real late and go straight to the bed. One night at twelve o'clock midnight the phone rang and I sat bolt upright in the bed. I didn't even need to pick up that phone. The NAACP dinner! When I answered the phone the organizer of the dinner told me that they had waited around, stomachs rumbling in chorus, until they finally gave me up and sent out for two hundred sandwiches from Hardee's drivethru. You've heard about somebody so low-down they could sit on a dime and swing their legs, well, that's about how I felt at that moment. I had had that bad dream for a long time, worrying that I would stand up a hundred or two church folk for a catering. That used to give me the cold sweats at night. Would you know, once it happened in real life I haven't thought about it since or messed up again since. But that doesn't mean that that chapter of the NAACP has ever used Weaver again either!

Those first few years had plenty of scrimping and setbacks. I just tried to keep remembering that song of Little Milton's, "We're Gonna Make It":

> We may have to fight hardships galore,
> but we gonna make it.
> I know we will.

After about year number five, I really felt that I was getting on solid ground. Come to find out later that all the business books and articles say that if you can hold out for five years . . . YOU'RE GONNA MAKE IT! So that old wise tale is true.

As soon as I felt I could, I decided to buy me a rental property. Back in the day I had lived in rental houses and apartments, and now I could afford to be a landlord my own self. Just like I had done by building my business one step at a time, I wanted to continue taking those baby steps into the future. Since I bought that first house in 1991, I have bought another here and there on the cheap. Remember Mr. Jerome buying that property at a county sale just for the taxes. That's where I learned that. Weaver is going to the next level!

Some people when they see a few zeroes on the bank statement rush out and get the biggest Mercedes that will fit in their driveway.

I have even seen the foreign cars parked outside double-wides. A satellite dish as big as a baby pool, a Mercedes the size of a school bus, and a double-wide. Now explain that so Weaver can understand it. I'm about taking care of mine and building, building, for the future twenty-years from now, not about trying to impress you at a thirty-second stoplight. Get out of here with your big Mercedes!

But because I have lived the rental lifestyle my own self, I take pride in my rental houses and fix them up just as nice as I do my own. I keep clean rentals with quality appliances fresh from out of the box, just like I live with myself. One of my rentals has a solid mahogany-wood front door on it. I do not even have a solid mahogany-wood front door on my *own* house. No matter how many rental houses I have or intend to get, I'm always going to be that way. You will never call me King D of the Ghetto.

Now the flip side of this is that if you sign on the dotted, that means you are going to keep my house clean and nice as if you owned it yourself. Do not call me at two o'clock A.M. in the morning to unclog your commode and out comes a hypo needle and all such stuff as that. Do not let me see you just stacking your garbage bags on the back porch so that every wildlife animal can get all up in 'em. Hefty does not make raccoon feeders, so just go on to the

Dempster Dumpster with your mess. If you do, I'll see to it that that leaking faucet gets repaired *right now!* You won't have to beg. And when your ceiling fan wears out, I'll get you the nice kind from Home Depot, just like in my own house. You are going to respect me just like I respect y'all.

The R.E.M. boys and all the folk who work with them had been coming in to Weaver D's Delicious Fine Foods pretty much since my opening in '86. When I say that I didn't pay them much mind that doesn't mean that I didn't think that they were real nice boys, 'cause I do and they are. Its just that I don't have time to be fawning and fanning over everybody that walks in the door when I have a restaurant to run.

A lot of R.E.M. fans came to the restaurant after the **Automatic for the People** CD came out. This is me in my office. I am always camera-ready.

Well, it wasn't too long after I got that first rental in 1991 that R.E.M. gave me a surprise when they sent somebody over to say that the band members liked my saying "Automatic for the People." It was immortalized on my sign from the Athens Fair days and they wanted to immortalize it again. Could they use it maybe as the title to their next album? (I call them albums, but today they are CDs, you know.) Well, that slogan is something that I mean sincerely and it has brought me happiness, so why not share it with the people? Yes, you can call that next R.E.M. album *Automatic for the People* and the best of luck to you and yours.

That album was released in 1992 and I will say from the get-go that I maybe didn't really know all about R.E.M. and how big they were. You know that Weaver is all about those groups like The Temptations and The Four Tops and The Supremes. But R.E.M. is just about the hugest group in the world. There are people in China listening to R.E.M. right now!

Warner Brothers Records had me make up bag after bag of my peanuts to ship all over the world to promote their album. We just took over the restaurant for days and days filling those seven thousand bags, roasting nuts, stamping the group's logo on the bag, filling the bag, folding the bag, stapling the bag, boxing the bag. Roasting, stamping, filling, folding, stapling, boxing—seven thousand times! We just took over the restaurant and it looked like Santa's workshop had blown up.

Just about the last night we were filling this humongous order, I got a telephone call telling me something I just never thought I'd hear. In the middle of all that fun with friends and family pitching in and The Temptations playing on the radio in the background, my cousin Jennifer Lane called to tell me we'd be burying my half-sister Wanda. Her van had been struck in Atlanta and she was killed in an instant.

Keeping our hands and minds busy really helped us through our shock and grieving. Lots of tears were shed, but the job got done. Weaver is automatic, automatic in good times and in bad. And if I have told somebody I will do a job, I will to my very best. Automatic.

I started getting requests from all over, I mean *all* over, for my signature Weaver D T-shirts—Germany, California, Italy, just everywhere. Because Weaver is always building, building, to that next level, I added a sideline of bumper stickers, license plates, car air fresheners, etc. You can get a bellyful of Weaver, put a Weaver T-shirt over it, and then drive it on home with a Weaver bumper sticker following you there. I have you covered.

I got calls from *Rolling Stone* magazine, *SPIN* magazine, *New Music Express* magazine, and I can't tell you how many other newspapers and TV stations. One reporter from the *Atlanta Journal-Constitution* asked me to name my favorite R.E.M. song. Not that I hadn't listened to their music, its just that I couldn't think of any R.E.M. songs *at that particular moment in time*, so I asked him to name me a couple. He reeled off a whole big long list of 'em until I remembered, "That's the one. That's my favorite." If a song is called "Shiny Happy People," it has *got* to be a good song.

People were coming from all around the world to eat my food and have their pictures taken under my sign and with my van that has my other slogan, "Quality Takes Time," on it. I have been down at the restaurant many a late night—I might leave some pork down there slow-cooking in the crock-pot—and as I leave there will be a whole gaggle of people there videoing my sign. That is why I must be camera-ready at all times.

One time I went to Weaver D's and there was an RV camper there and the lady of the house was busy filming my outside.

I said, "How y'all doing? Come in! I'm Weaver D. Automatic!"

She said, "We so glad to see you. We know this is not the time y'all usually are open, but my husband and I were passing through Georgia and my children made us get on the other highway to come into Athens. We're on our way to New York."

They were Austrian.

I said, "Y'all, I ain't got no food or anything ready. I just came down here to get tomorrow's pork out of the crock-pot."

They started buying the Weaver D T-shirts, the auto tags, the glasses, the coffee mugs, the coozies. That bunch bought about a hundred dollars worth of Weaver D marketing items.

One time a girl came in from Italy and before she even stepped across the threshold she was like, "*Ahhowww*."

And I said, "Sister, you all right?"

She went off fully charged, "*Owww*, I heard about it, I read about it, and I'm *here!*" She hopped across that threshold like she was jumping the broom.

I said, "Are you O.K.?"

"*Owww.*"

She just went *off!*

Sometimes when people come in the restaurant I take their order and give them their change with only a thank-you. They just keep standing there. Miss Betty is halfway finished plating up their food and they are still standing at the register. They'll say, "But you didn't say 'Automatic.'" And sometimes when I say "Automatic" to a customer they'll whisper to whoever they're with, "I *told* you he would say it."

That October of '92 was a big month. There was a giant record release party to celebrate the album and to raise money for one of R.E.M.'s favorite local charities, Community Connection, and I catered the food. All the hits from the restaurant, crowder peas, fried chicken, squash casserole, and Michael Stipe's favorite, sweet potato soufflé. Do you know that his mother called me the next day to thank me for doing that party? That is Southern manners for you.

Later that month Al Gore came to town to talk about him and Bill Clinton being president and in his stump speech he said, "George Bush is 'Out of Time.' Bill Clinton and Al Gore are going to be *Automatic for the People.*"

We just couldn't believe my "Automatic for the People" sign was taken right off the building. It was returned with a guilty letter four days later.

Finally, Halloween week, my sign was stolen. Stolen right off the building. I was just real upset, because this was my claim to fame. But somebody's mama had done a good job because on the fifth of November my sign got returned with a letter of apology and a ten-dollar bill. This is the letter that was in a Baggie taped to the sign:

Weaver D:

Sorry for the terrible inconvenience over the past week. Upon further thought, the idea of possessing a genuine piece of Athens history became a guilt-felt burden. Enclosed is a small borrowing fee, which will hopefully cover any hardware replacement cost. Thank you for the opportunity of a lifetime.

Your biggest fan

Now in the middle of all this craziness, you know my restaurant wasn't gonna run itself. I decided to take chitlins off the menu because I just didn't have the time to be messing with them. I've told you before how much it takes to clean 'em and all. I know now I should have seen it coming, but there was a customer backlash. Some of my regular customers got real upset with Weaver D's and they wrote up a petition. This is what it said:

THE CHITLIN PETITION

To the Proprietor of Weaver D's Delicious Fine Foods:

We, the concerned and suffering citizens of Athens, wish to voice our opinion concerning the recent notice that your fine establishment is no longer serving chitlins. We are *highly* upset and disappointed!!! May we suggest that you prepare enough only for us regulars and not the clients who come simply because they think they'll get in a video? We hope this letter will do the trick and we won't have to take other action, such as a protest march in front of your restaurant! Get those chitlins cookin'. Thanking you in advance,

Then it was signed by a whole passel of my regular customers.

I'm a businessman. I hear you. Those three exclamation points are *serious*. I try to have chitlins every chance I get. Chitlins are just really time-consuming. Now, I can clean a bucket of chitlins, ten pounds, in one hour. I can clean that much easy, but ten pounds ain't going nowhere. You could probably sell two to three orders out of it and you'd have to charge seven dollars an order. Unless you have the labor for somebody to just stand back there in the kitchen and chitlin-clean all day, it's just not worth it.

It's one or two folk around here that say, "D, I don't eat anybody's chitlins but my own and yours, 'cause I want to make sure they're clean. And I know you're clean." Sometimes I sit right there in the dining room of the restaurant and I have my little bucket and my little bowl for clean chitlins and I have my trash can to accept that little fatty skin you have to take off. People will come in and say, "*Ooob*, that's the way to do it." But one day a lady came in saying, "Oh, D, you throwing away too much by taking off that skin like that." But I'm getting all that stuff offa there. I'm not just gonna pick the fat and the little corn out and call it clean. It *all* has to go.

Some people don't like chitlins. One time I overheard a lady in the restaurant say, "I don't eat no chitlins."

Her husband said, "Didn't you eat a pork sausage for breakfast just this morning?"

"Yeah," she said.

"Well, you eat chitlins then," he said.

Having my slogan out on a CD brought a lot of good things to Weaver, business and attention and a lot of friendly customers from around the world. Like I told you in the beginning I even got to go to the Grammys with my half-sister Tamara. Me wearing a mink jacket and her wearing her purple fox stole that she bought at the same store where Rick James and Diana Ross shop.

Even though that is a big wave to ride, I still had a business to run day to day. I've always worked hard and even during the high heights of the R.E.M. stuff I continued to work hard. Amidst all the fun and excitement, I knew that I had to keep the lights on and the doors open. The lady at Southern Bell telephone does not accept Grammys ticket stubs as payment. For real. I just kept working and building, building. When I treated myself to the first vacation I'd had in thirteen years, my friend Didi said she saw me "sleep-working," asleep in my hotel room in Freeport, Bahamas, washing a big pile of dishes. So, whatever the rewards, day to day I still strive to be, you know what I'm going to say, automatic.

HOW YOU CAN GET AUTOMATIC TOO

→ 9 ←

**Time to graduate
with a Ph.D. in Weaver D.**

→HOW do I sum up what I've summed up? You say you want
to be automatic just like Weaver. That is understandable.
Getting automatic has given me a blessed life, full of the
love of my big family and of friends from all over the world.
Even though I've traveled some rocky roads—you already
read chapter five, so you know what time it is—those bad
times have fallen behind me, I have *released* them! And do
you know that whenever I have released my grip on hard

times, I've found my hand open to receive new blessings. Let me break it down so that even a child could understand. Here are the four habits of highly automatic people.

Automatic Point **#1**

WORK AUTOMATIC!

Have you been to Stuckey's or the five-and-dimes and seen those plants they sell that you never have to feed or water?

Servin' it up at Weaver D's Delicious Fine Foods. I was voted best fried chicken in Athens two years running.

Those little ferns live on nothing but air and driftwood. If you can read this, you are not an air fern, friend, and that means you have got to do more than sit around and breathe. You need four walls and three squares, and that means you have got to work. I don't pay my employees to sit around on their driftwood soaking up my free air. Think about it from my point of view. Unless you are pulling more ducats through the front door of Weaver D's than you are being paid, you are an asssitter, not an asset. That's just how it is, straight up. You are a nice person and Weaver wishes you well, but you have got to come on with the come-on. Don't think you can just show up, clock in, and zone out. Weaver D's is a money-making restaurant, not a day care.

But having that attitude will work in your favor too. If you don't have that nine-to-five thing goin' on, you will be living with your auntie, putting your Bell South bill in your mama's name, sneaking on the bus with yesterday's ticket—you will not be free. Although I have had hard times, like Mother I have always worked to make my life better. Now many years later we can go where we want, buy what we want, live where we want. If your top two financial institutions are your mama's cookie jar and the check-cashing place, you need to get yourself a J-O-B.

Automatic Point **#2**

KEEP AUTOMATIC!

I started out many years ago making those delivery meat-and-three dinners for sororities and fraternities. For a long time that income sustained me and helped me save up to build my dreams. Now I have my own restaurant, a big catering business, and rental houses and investments. But even after lo these many years, I go back to those Greeks whenever they give me a call and commence to dishin' the soul. That's how I started out and if Weaver D's burned to the ground tomorrow I know I could keep body and soul together with just those sorority and fraternity gigs. That's called staying the course. Now matter what you do in business, what new things you try, how far you reach, keep on with the basics. You'll take bigger leaps if you know that solid bedrock is waiting for you to land on.

Automatic Point **#3**

BELIEVE AUTOMATIC!

Now concentrate on this next part 'cause I am fixing to go heavy on you. There is no reason why you have to ride around in a raggedy-ass car with a "Honk If You Love Jesus" bumper sticker on the back. Why did God create you if He didn't want you to be happy? Happy every which way. He wants you to be happy in your community and in your home life and in your church life *and* in your work life. But don't think you can just sit in a pew with your little church suit on, gum your way through a hymn, and tithe some loose buttons and pocket lint into the collection plate and think that the abundance will set to flowing—you know that's what Evangelist Diggs called "playing church." You have got to truly believe that your hopes and dreams are what God wants for you and that He wants to make you happy. But don't be thinking that I'm guilty of what my Holiness wife Maxine Underwood said I was, that I worshiped my house—a pile of bricks and mortar—and my car—a heap of tin and paint. I know that all things in His kingdom belong to Him to bestow or to take away, but while I'm here I'm surely going to say, "Thank you, Jesus, your loaner car rides real nice!"

Automatic Point **#4**

LIVE AUTOMATIC!

I know a man who is real depressing. Never talks to anybody. Says his long-distance is too expensive, his grandbabies talk too loud, his preacher talks too soft, and his wife talks too much, period. He just sits there in silence, sits there year after year. He doesn't want to die, but looks to me like he doesn't want to live either.

One of the things I loved most about Mr. Jerome was that he was never stingy. When you went to his and Fanny Maud's house you *knew* you would get your feed on and that the Johnny Walker and VO would flow. The Mosbys were lucky that they had the money to do that, but it all stemmed from their generous spirits. The man I talking about here is just stingy with his *spirit*. He is not giving of himself, not to his wife, not to his children, and I'll bet not to God either.

Mother and me at our Customer Appreciation in December 1998. We'd been open for a lucky thirteen years. We had a choir and a DJ.

So, what is Weaver summing up for you? *Come out of that coma and get out there and do something!* Get out there and make a mudpie and cry over English peas and eat a tomato still warm from the Georgia sun. Jump double Dutch and have a pig ear sandwich and fill your "treasure chest." Iron your whitest shirt and put on your shiniest shoes and do The Bump with a big-butted girl. Hug your mama hard and speak in tongues and make a batch of collards for some scruffy musicians. Get out there and be like my Go-Anywhere, Do-Anything Beetle.

Are you feeling it yet? Are you feeling automatic? With so many joys in this world and more we can't imagine in the next, how can you not be—

Automatic!

RECIPES

"*Quality Takes Time*"

—DEXTER WEAVER

Fruit Punch

serves 35

2 (4-ounce) packages tropical
   punch Kool-Aid®
1 (4-ounce) package raspberry-
   cranberry Kool-Aid®
1 (4-ounce) package strawberry
   Kool-Aid®
2 cups sugar
32 ounces reconstituted
   lemon juice
1 (20-ounce) can crushed
   pineapple
1 3/4 gallons ice water

Mix dry ingredients in large
punch bowl. Add a small
amount of lemon juice to dissolve powder; add remaining
lemon juice, crushed pineapple,
and water. Stir all ingredients
thoroughly.

**Put some of the punch in a fluted
bundt pan or decorative mold and
freeze solid. Float the ice ring in
the punch.**

Sweet Iced Tea

serves 10 to 12

3 family-sized tea bags
2 cups cold water
1 cup sugar

Put water in a saucepan and
add tea bags. Bring to a boil
and immediately remove from
heat. Add sugar and stir to
dissolve. Allow to steep 10 to
15 minutes before removing
tea bags. Pour into a pitcher
and add 8 cups of water.

**If your tea tends to come out
bitter, put a small pinch of baking
soda in the water when you add
the sugar.**

Cornmeal Muffins

makes 1 dozen

1 1/3 cups self-rising white cornmeal
1 tablespoon sugar
1 1/3 cups buttermilk
1/4 cup unsalted butter, melted
1 large egg, lightly beaten

Preheat oven to 425° F.

Combine cornmeal and sugar in medium mixing bowl; make well
in center of mixture.

Combine buttermilk, butter, and egg; add to dry ingredients,
stirring until smooth.

Spoon into greased muffin tins, filling tins 2/3 full.

Bake in oven for 20 minutes or until golden brown.

Buttermilk Biscuits

serves 10

1 1/2 cups all-purpose flour
1 tablespoon baking powder
1/4 teaspoon baking soda
1 tablespoon sugar
1/2 teaspoon salt
1/2 cup vegetable shortening,
or half and half quantity of shortening and butter
1/4 to 1/3 cup buttermilk
2 tablespoons melted butter

Preheat oven to 400° F.

Sift together dry ingredients into large mixing bowl. Cut in
shortening until it forms pea-sized granules.

Make a well in the center of the flour mixture and mix in enough
buttermilk to hold dough together.

Turn onto a well-floured board and roll into a 3/4-inch square.

Dip the open end of a jelly jar into flour and use to cut as many
biscuits as possible from the square.

Place 1/2 inch apart on an ungreased cookie sheet. Brush the tops
with butter and bake 13 to 15 minutes, until golden brown.

Serve warm.

Baked Chicken Salad

serves 10 to 12

This recipe yields a lot. Once you taste it you'll be glad you made so much. The salad is even better the next day.

15 pieces chicken
1 medium white onion, sliced
1/2 tablespoon salt
1/2 tablespoon freshly ground black pepper
2 garlic cloves, finely minced
1/2 tablespoon seasoned salt
1/4 bunch celery, chopped
1 1/2 ounces salad cubes or pickle relish
6 hard-boiled eggs, sliced
1/2 quart mayonnaise (more or less, to taste)

Preheat oven to 350° F.

Wash chicken thoroughly and gently pay dry between tea towels. Spread onion slices in baking dish. Place chicken on top of onion; add salt, pepper, garlic, and seasoned salt.

Bake chicken in oven for 1 to 1 1/2 hours, or until meat falls from the bone. Drain chicken; allow to come to room temperature. Cut or shred chicken, according to preference.

Add celery, salad cubes, eggs, and mayonnaise. Mix thoroughly.

Baked Mushroom Chicken

serves 8

8 split chicken breasts (leave skin on)
2 medium onions, sliced
1 (10 3/4 ounces) can cream of mushroom soup
1 (10 3/4 ounces) can cream of celery soup
Worcestershire sauce to taste
salt and freshly ground black pepper to taste

Preheat oven to 350° F.

Wash chicken, pat dry between tea towels. Place chicken bone-down in glass baking dish. Add salt and pepper to taste. Add onions, soup, and three or more dashes Worcestershire sauce.

Cover with foil; punch four sets of fork holes to allow steam to escape.

Bake 1 1/2 to 2 hours.

Try serving this chicken over rice with garden peas, green salad, and hot buttered rolls.

Cornish Game Hens

serves 8

4 Cornish game hens
1 large white onion, thickly sliced
1 stick unsalted butter or margarine
1 teaspoon poultry seasoning
2 garlic cloves, crushed
2 teaspoons salt
1 teaspoon freshly ground black pepper
large oven bag

Preheat oven to 350° F.

Remove neck, liver, etc. from hens and save for stock or giblet gravy.

Wash hens thoroughly.

Place hens in a large oven bag.

Add all other ingredients; close bag.

Bake in oven for 2 hours.

Cut hens in half prior to serving.

Barbecued Pork Roast

serves 16

1 8-pound Boston butt pork roast
2 teaspoons salt
2 teaspoons freshly ground black pepper
3 teaspoons garlic, finely minced
1 teaspoon seasoned salt
1 batch Automatic barbecue sauce

Preheat oven to 350° F.

Place pork roast in baking dish.

Season with salt, pepper, and garlic.

Add salt, pepper, garlic, and seasoned salt and coat with sauce.

Bake for 2 1/2 hours, basting with sauce as needed.

Allow to cool 30 minutes before pulling meat from the bone and
adding barbecue sauce to taste.

**Serve with bread, coleslaw, and baked beans. This will make great sand-
wiches the next day.**

Automatic Barbecue Sauce

6 tablespoons vegetable or
olive oil
3 large white onions,
thickly sliced
3 garlic cloves, minced
3 cups ketchup
3/4 cup red wine vinegar
3/4 cup packed dark
brown sugar
3 tablespoons Dijon mustard
6 tablespoons Worcestershire
sauce

Sauté onion and garlic in oil
until tender, about 5 minutes. Add remaining ingredients and cook over low
heat for 10 minutes.

**Use this for baking chicken, beef,
or pork. Its strong enough to
stand up to grilled meats too.**

Spare Ribs
serves 6 to 8

2 3- to 4-pound rack of ribs,
well trimmed of excess fat
3-4 garlic cloves, crushed
1 teaspoon salt
1 tablespoon freshly
ground pepper
1 large white onion,
thickly sliced
1 batch Automatic
barbecue sauce

Preheat oven to 350° F.
Thoroughly wash ribs and cut
between bones with a
cleaver.
Season ribs with garlic, salt,
and pepper.
Slice onion and place in bottom of baking dish.
Place ribs on top of onion and
coat with barbecue sauce.
Bake in oven for 2 hours, or
until meat just begins to fall
from the bone, basting with
sauce as needed.

Chittlins

serves 4-5

1 (10-pound) bucket of chittlins
1 large white onion, chopped
1 jalapeño or fingerhot pepper
1 tablespoon salt
1 tablespoon freshly ground black pepper
2 tablespoons white vinegar
10 cups water

Clean chittlins thoroughly.
Wash 3 to 4 times in cold water.
Pour water into large stockpot and add chittlins.
Add remaining ingredients.
Cook on medium heat for 2 1/2 hours, until tender.

Robert Lee's Pork Chops and Potatoes Special
serves 6

6 pork loin chops
1 teaspoon garlic salt
1 teaspoon salt
1 teaspoon freshly
ground pepper
7 white or baking potatoes,
thickly sliced
1 3/4 cup water
3/4 stick unsalted butter or
margarine

Season chops with garlic salt, salt, and pepper. Place in frying pan with 1 cup water. Cook on medium heat for 15 minutes. Peel and slice potatoes; place on top of chops. Add butter or margarine and 3/4 cup water.

Cook on medium heat for an additional 1 to 1 1/2 hours, turning over after 30 minutes.

Barbecued Lamb Chops
serves 12

12 to 16 lamb chops
1 large white onion, sliced
1 teaspoon salt
1 tablespoon freshly ground
black pepper
3 tablespoons garlic,
finely minced
1 teaspoon seasoned salt
1 batch Automatic
barbecue sauce

Preheat oven to 350° F.
Slice onion and place in baking dish. Place lamb chops on top of onion.
Add salt, pepper, garlic, and seasoning salt and coat with sauce.
Bake for 2 hours, or until meat begins to separate from the bone, basting with sauce as needed.

Tender as a Mother's Love Chuck Roast

serves 10

This recipe serves 10, 6 if they're hungry.

1 (10-pound) boneless beef chuck roast
4 to 6 cloves garlic, crushed
1 large white onion, thickly sliced
10 medium white potatoes
2 pounds carrots, peeled and thickly sliced
6 ounces white mushrooms
2 teaspoons salt
1 tablespoon freshly ground black pepper
2 tablespoons Worcestershire sauce
3 bay leaves
1 teaspoon dried thyme, crumbled
1 teaspoon dried oregano, crumbled
6 cups water

Pour water into Dutch oven or stockpot.
Add chuck roast, onion, salt, pepper, and crushed garlic.
Cook on medium heat for 2 hours.
Add thickly-sliced carrots and potatoes.
Cook for 45 additional minutes or until done.

Corned Beef Hash
serves 12

This is a good way to doctor-up canned corned beef.

2 (12-ounce) cans of corned beef
1 large white onion, finely chopped
1 large tomato, peeled and chopped
5 tablespoons vegetable shortening
6 ounces tomato paste
1 teaspoon salt
1 teaspoon freshly ground pepper
1/2 cup water

Sauté onion and tomato in shortening in frying pan.
Season with salt and pepper.
Add corned beef; mix thoroughly.
Add water.
Cook on low heat for 10 minutes.
Add tomato paste.
Cook for 10 additional minutes.

**Serve corned beef hash over a bed of steamed white rice or with mashed
potatoes on the side.**

Oxtails
serves 8

4 to 6 pounds oxtails,
well trimmed
1 tablespoon salt
1 teaspoon freshly ground black pepper
1 teaspoon garlic salt
1/2 teaspoon seasoned salt
1 large white onion, thickly sliced
6 cups beef broth or water
1 teaspoon cider vinegar

Thoroughly rinse meat. Season meat with salt, pepper, garlic salt, and seasoned salt. Place oxtails and onions in large heavy stockpot. Add water and vinegar. Cook on medium-high heat 2 1/2 to 3 hours, or until oxtails are tender and water has reduced to gravy.

To avoid mushiness, remove from heat before meat falls off the bone. Serve over white rice, boiled new potatoes, or buttered egg noodles.

Spaghetti Pie

serves 6

6 ounces spaghetti
2 tablespoons unsalted butter
1/3 cup Parmesan cheese
2 large eggs, well beaten
1 cup cottage cheese
1 pound ground round
1/2 cup white onion, chopped
1/4 cup green pepper, seeded
and chopped

1 (8-ounce) can whole
tomatoes
6 ounces tomato paste
1/2 tablespoon sugar
1 tablespoon dried oregano
1/2 tablespoon garlic salt
1/2 cup mozzarella cheese,
shredded

Preheat oven to 350°

Brown beef in frying pan with onion and green pepper; drain and
set aside.

Boil spaghetti until barely tender and drain thoroughly. Put
spaghetti in medium mixing bowl and stir in butter, Parmesan
cheese, and eggs.

Spray 10-inch pie pan with baking spray. Form spaghetti into a
crust in pie plate. Spread cottage cheese over spaghetti crust.

Combine undrained tomatoes, tomato paste, sugar, oregano, and
garlic salt in medium saucepan over low heat. Heat until
warmed through; add beef and pour into crust.

Bake uncovered for 20 minutes.

Sprinkle with mozzarella cheese and bake until cheese bubbles
and is lightly browned.

Roast Beef
serves 12 to 15

1 (7-pound) beef roast
1 large white onion, chopped
1/2 tablespoon garlic salt
1 teaspoon salt
1/2 teaspoon seasoned salt
1 teaspoon freshly ground
black pepper

Preheat oven to 350° F.
Slice onion and place on
bottom of baking dish.
Place beef roast on top of
onion.
Rub with seasonings.
Bake for 2 hours, or until done.

Cream Tuna on Toast
serves 4

**Memorize this recipe. It is good to
make after a hard day of work
because all the ingredients are
right there in your pantry.
Automatic.**

1 (12-ounce) can chunk light
tuna in spring water or oil
1 (10 3/4-ounce) can cream of
mushroom soup
1/2 teaspoon salt
1/2 teaspoon freshly ground
black pepper
1 tablespoon water
8 slices sandwich bread,
toasted

Toast bread.
Pour soup into saucepan;
bring to simmer. Add
drained tuna, salt, pepper,
and water.
Get back up to a low simmer.
Simmer for 10 minutes.
Serve over toast.

Seafood Gumbo

serves 10-12

2 small white onions, sliced
1/2 stick unsalted butter
1/8 cup all-purpose flour
1 quart chicken stock
1 1/4 cups cooked tomatoes
1/2 pound okra, both tips removed
1/2 cup chopped celery
1/2 teaspoon dried thyme
1 to 2 sprigs parsley
1 bay leaf
1 cup lump crabmeat, picked over for cartilage
12 large shrimp, peeled and deveined
12 oysters, shucked
salt and freshly ground pepper to taste

Melt butter in frying pan.

Add onions and sauté until soft.

Add flour; cook on low to medium heat for 5 minutes.

Add all remaining ingredients except shrimp and oysters.

Simmer for 1 hour, then add shrimp and oysters.

Simmer for 10 additional minutes, or until done.

Crab and Barley Soup
serves 10

1 dozen soft-shell crabs, claws and all
1 pound lump crabmeat, picked over for cartilage
1 1/2 thick-cut bacon strips
1 1/2 cups fresh vegetables of your choice (string beans, carrots, cabbage, etc.)
6 ounces whole peeled tomatoes
1/2 cup medium barley

Fry bacon, drain on paper towels, and crumble.

Put crabs in large stockpot of water with vegetables, and tomatoes.

Cook on low heat for four hours. At the third hour, add barley.

When almost done, add crab meat and bacon.

Leave on low heat until crab meat begins to flake.

Remove crabs and serve on side.

Baltimore Crab Dressing

serves 8-10

1 pound lump crabmeat, picked over for cartilage
1 cup mayonnaise
1 cup condensed milk
1/2 medium onion, finely chopped
1 or 2 stalks chopped celery, finely chopped
1/4 cup dried bread crumbs
1 tablespoon seafood seasoning
1/2 teaspoon parsley, finely minced
1/2 stick unsalted butter
1 teaspoon paprika

Preheat oven to 300° F.

Combine all ingredients except butter and paprika in bowl; mix
   thoroughly.

Transfer to baking dish.

Dot top with sliced butter and sprinkle with paprika.

Bake for 1 hour.

For best results, refrigerate overnight, then bring to room
   temperature before serving.

Submitted by Aunt Bennie Hanson of Baltimore, Maryland.

Weaver D's Seasoning Mix
makes 4 cups

Just like you have got to have the right tools when you are building a
house, you have got to have all the right tools when you make a meal.
Lay out all your ingredients and equipment right there at your fingertips.
You shouldn't be walking around like Moses in the desert every time you
need a measuring cup. Measure out all the ingredients. You do not want
to be caught with your hand all upside a chicken and discover that there
is not a drop of paprika in the house.

3 1/2 cups all-purpose flour
3 tablespoons garlic salt
3 tablespoons seasoned salt
3 tablespoons freshly ground black pepper
1 tablespoon salt

Mix all ingredients thoroughly in medium bowl.
Store in an airtight container.

Use this mix to for delicious batter-fried chicken and pork chops. It will
batter about 3 to 4 pounds of fryer pieces. Sprinkle with seasoned salt
just before serving.

Mother's Baked Beans

serves 6 to 8

This is a favorite at family get-togethers and covered-dish suppers at church. The recipe is easily halved or doubled.

1 pound dried navy beans, picked over and rinsed
1 tablespoon vegetable oil
1/4 cup firmly packed dark brown sugar
2 tablespoons Grade B maple syrup
1 cup ketchup
8 ounces smoked link sausage, thinly sliced
1 large green bell pepper, seeded and chopped
1 medium onion, finely chopped
1 tablespoon dried oregano or 2 tablespoons fresh

In large mixing bowl, cover beans with 2 inches of water and soak overnight. Drain and rinse beans in a colander and transfer to a heavy 4-quart saucepan. Cover beans with 3 inches of water and simmer covered 1 hour or until tender. Drain beans reserving 2 cups of the cooking liquid.

Combine oil, brown sugar, maple syrup, and ketchup and mix well. Combine syrup mixture with beans and remaining ingredients in a large kettle.

Cook covered for 3 to 5 hours until beans are very tender. Add reserved cooking liquid as needed.

Pole Beans

Vegetables & Side Dishes

serves 8

In the summertime, there are fresh produce stands all along country roads. Shake hands with the man who grew your beans.

1 1/2 to 2 pounds smoked
pork neckbones
1/4 pound fatback
2 1/2 pounds pole beans,
strings removed and
snapped in half
1 medium white onion,
thickly sliced
1/2 teaspoon salt
1/2 teaspoon freshly ground
black pepper
4 cups water

Pour water in saucepan.
Add smoked neckbones
and fatback and simmer for
1 hour.
Add beans, onion, salt, and
pepper.
Simmer for 1 hour.

Broccoli with Cheese

serves 4

1 bunch broccoli,
separated into florets
1/2 teaspoon salt
1/2 teaspoon freshly ground
black pepper
8 ounces sharp Cheddar
cheese, freshly shredded
1/4 stick unsalted butter
1 tablespoon whole milk

In small saucepan over low
heat, combine cheese,
butter, and milk. Stir
constantly to melt cheese.
Boil or steam broccoli for 10
to 20 minutes until tender.
Drain well and add salt and
pepper.
Pour over broccoli.

Vegetables & Side Dishes

Boiled Cabbage
serves 10 to 12

1 large green cabbage
1 small white onion, sliced
1 small red bell pepper,
    seeded and diced
2 stalks celery, chopped
2 tablespoons salt
1 teaspoon freshly ground
    pepper
4 cups water

Put all ingredients in heavy
    saucepan of boiling water
    to cover.
Simmer for 15 to 20 minutes
    or until tender, being sure
    to not overcook.

**Because there are no dripping
items of any sort in this recipe, it
makes for a great vegetarian dish.
Serve with The Best Pepper
Vinegar or hot pepper sauce.**

The Best Pepper Vinegar
makes 1 1/2 cups

6 ounces small red or green
hot chiles (cayenne or tabasco)
1 1/2 cups distilled
    white vinegar
1/4 teaspoon salt
pinch of ground cayenne

Pack well-washed and towel-
    dried chiles into thoroughly
    sterilized canning jar.
Combine remaining ingredi-
    ents in small bowl and stir
    until salt dissolves.
Pour over chiles and seal
    canning jar.
Let vinegar stand at room
    temperature at least 3 weeks
    and up to 6 months.

**Use this to doctor-up greens,
stews, and vegetables.**

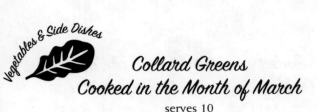

Collard Greens
Cooked in the Month of March
serves 10

Collards that are grown during fall and winter months are tender from
fresh-fallen dew, so they may cook more rapidly than normal.
Take care not to overcook.

1 ham hock (about 1 1/4 pounds)
1/2 pound fatback
3 pounds collard greens, preferably with small leaves
2 tablespoons salt
1/2 tablespoon sugar
6 cups water

Wash greens 5 times or until grit is entirely gone
Pour water into large saucepan or stockpot.
Add ham hock and fatback; cook on medium heat for 1 hour.
Remove stems and coarse ribs from collards and discard.
Cut greens into 3-inch slices;
Add collards, salt, and sugar to fat.
Cook over medium heat for 2 hours or until tender,
   stirring occasionally.

Serve with The Best Pepper Vinegar or hot pepper sauce.

Turnip Greens

serves 6

The season for turnip greens runs right through till Christmas.
Always buy the youngest, most tender greens you can find.
Don't get those old yellow, withered-up leaves.

5 pounds turnip greens
2 pieces smoked pork neckbones
1 pound fatback
2 tablespoons salt

Wash greens 5 times or until grit is entirely gone.

Remove stems and coarse ribs from greens and discard.

Cut greens into 3-inch slices.

Place neckbone and fatback in pot with water.

Cook on medium heat for 45 minutes.

Add greens and cook over medium heat for 2 hours or until
  tender, stirring occasionally.

Serve with hot pepper sauce or pickled peaches.

Cucumbers in Sour Cream

serves 8 to 10

2 to 3 English seedless cucumbers (or 6 to 8 Kirby cucumbers),
peeled and thinly sliced
3/4 tablespoon coarse kosher salt
2 tablespoons minced white onion or shallot
1 tablespoon freshly squeezed lemon juice, strained
1/2 cup sour cream
1 tablespoon fresh dill, finely chopped
1/2 teaspoon salt
1/2 teaspoon freshly ground black pepper

Place cucumbers in colander; sprinkle with kosher salt. Put
colander in a slightly larger bowl or let stand in sink to drain
for 30 minutes.

Rinse off the salt and gently pat cucumber slices dry between tea
towels. Put cucumbers in a medium mixing bowl.

Mix remaining ingredients in a small mixing bowl and stir into
cucumber slices.

Refrigerate for at least 1 hour before serving.

Cornbread Dressing

serves 40

**If you are expecting Weavers for dinner, make the whole recipe!
Otherwise, it can easily be halved.**

12 to 15 cornbread muffins
12 slices white bread
1/2 large white onion, diced
1/4 bunch celery, chopped
2 (14 1/2-ounce) cans chicken broth
2 teaspoons rubbed sage
1 1/2 teaspoons poultry seasoning
1 1/4 stick unsalted butter, melted
1 1/4 stick margarine, melted
3 large eggs, beaten

Preheat oven to 350° F.

Tear muffins and bread into small pieces into a large mixing
bowl.

Combine and mix all ingredients except butter and margarine.

Add butter and margarine to 13 x 9 x 3 baking dish; add mixture.

Bake in oven for 1 hour.

Fried Corn
serves 10

6 ears yellow corn
1 tablespoon bacon drippings
1 teaspoon sugar
1/4 cup all-purpose flour
1 teaspoon salt
1/2 teaspoon freshly ground black pepper
1/2 stick unsalted butter or margarine
1 1/4 cups water

Cut corn off cobs, being sure to scrape cobs thoroughly.

Pour bacon drippings into frying pan.

Mix corn, sugar, flour, salt, pepper, and water in large bowl.

Pour mixture into frying pan.

Cook on low to medium heat for 45 minutes or until done, stirring often to prevent sticking.

Melt butter or margarine over corn before serving.

Add more soul by using fatback instead of bacon drippings. Slice fatback and fry until crispy. Then remove fatback and partially drain the pan, leaving a small amount of grease for the corn to fry in. Serve fried fatback on the side. Some people will eat 2 servings because it's so good.

Carrie Jackson's
Corn Pudding
serves 10 to 12

4 (4 3/4 ounce) cans sweet cream-style corn
4 large eggs, beaten
1/2 cup whole milk
1/2 teaspoon freshly ground black pepper
1/2 teaspoon salt
2 1/2 tablespoons all-purpose flour
1/2 cup sugar
3/4 stick unsalted butter or margarine
1/2 tablespoon vanilla extract
1/2 teaspoon lemon extract

Preheat oven to 350° F.
Beat eggs.
Add milk, pepper, and salt; set aside.
Pour corn into large mixing bowl.
Add flour and sugar; stir well.
Combine milk and egg mixture with corn mixture.
Add vanilla and lemon extracts; mix thoroughly.
Transfer to a 2 x 9 x 12-inch glass baking dish.
Dot top of mixture with sliced butter or margarine.
Bake for 1 hour and 15 minutes.

The Three-Cheese
Mac 'n' Cheese
serves 8 to 10

**What is soul food? If you have to ask, you have not had
Weaver D's mac 'n' cheese.**

1 pound macaroni noodles
6 ounces sharp Cheddar cheese, shredded
6 ounces mild Cheddar cheese, shredded
6 ounces mozzarella cheese, shredded
1 tablespoon freshly ground black pepper
1 large egg, beaten
1 1/2 cups whole milk
1/4 stick unsalted butter
1/8 stick margarine

Preheat oven to 350° F.

Boil macaroni until barely tender; drain and pour into large glass
   baking dish.

Add cheese and pepper; stir.

Combine eggs and milk; pour over macaroni.

Top with sliced butter and margarine.

Bake for 1 hour or until bubbly.

Potato Salad

serves 10 to 15

For best flavor and texture, be sure to add ingredients to potatoes while the potatoes are still warm.

10 pounds white or Idaho potatoes, peeled and sliced
10 large eggs
2 tablespoons salt
2 teaspoons freshly ground black pepper
1/2 bunch celery, chopped
1 quart mayonnaise
2 tablespoons mild yellow mustard
8 ounces salad cubes or pickle relish

Boil potatoes in a large stockpot on medium heat for 20 minutes or until fork easily pierces them.

While potatoes are boiling, boil eggs in a separate saucepan for 8 to 10 minutes; drain and peel under cool running water while peeling them. Chop eggs into medium-size chunks.

Drain potatoes and allow to cool for 20 minutes.

Add eggs, celery, mayonnaise, mustard, and salad cubes or pickle relish to potatoes. Add salt and pepper to taste.

Mix thoroughly. Refrigerate for 1 to 2 hours before serving.

Squash Casserole
serves 8 to 10

4 pounds yellow or summer squash, cut into 1/4-inch slices
2 tablespoons unsalted butter or margarine, melted
1 large white onion, finely chopped
2 cloves garlic, pressed
1 (10 3/4-ounce) can cream of mushroom soup
1 cup sharp Cheddar or Colby Longhorn cheese, freshly shredded
2 large eggs, beaten
1 teaspoon salt
1/2 teaspoon freshly ground black pepper

Preheat oven to 350° F.

Cook squash in boiling water to cover 8 to 10 minutes or until
   tender.

Drain squash; gently press between tea towels.

In large skillet, sauté onion and garlic in butter until tender.

Combine onions, garlic, squash, and remaining ingredients; mix
   thoroughly.

Spoon mixture into lightly greased 11 x 7 x 1 1/2-inch
   baking dish.

Bake in oven for 30 minutes or until bubbly.

Fried Squash

serves 8 to 10

1 1/2 pounds yellow or summer squash, sliced into thick coins
1 large white onion, coarsely chopped
3 strips thickly cut smoked bacon
1 teaspoon salt
1 teaspoon freshly ground black pepper

Fry bacon in frying pan over medium heat and remove; leave drippings in pan.
Add squash and onions.
Season with salt and pepper.
Cook on medium heat for 30 minutes.

Make this a vegetarian stir-fry by using vegetable oil instead of bacon drippings. Sprinkle with chopped parsley, rosemary, sage, or chervil.

Stewed Okra

serves 6 to 8

Stewed okra is delicious. To avoid the famous okra sliminess, don't overcook.

1 pound small fresh okra
1 large yellow onion, sliced
1/2 stick unsalted butter
2 ripe tomatoes, coarsely chopped
1 teaspoon salt
1/2 teaspoon freshly ground black pepper

Cut tips off each end of okra pods. Blanch in boiling water for 4 to 5 minutes. Drain well.
In a large skillet, sauté the onion in the butter until softened, about 5 minutes. Stir in tomatoes, okra, salt, and pepper.
Simmer 10 minutes.

Sweet Potato Soufflé
serves 6 to 8

R.E.M.'s Michael Stipe is a fan of this side dish.

6 small sweet potatoes (about 3 pounds), peeled and cut into
small chunks
3/4 cup sugar
3 large eggs, lightly beaten
1/2 cup unsalted butter or margarine, melted
3 tablespoons whole milk
2 teaspoons freshly grated nutmeg
2 teaspoons vanilla extract
3/4 teaspoon lemon extract

Preheat oven to 350° F.

Cook sweet potatoes in boiling water to cover 15 to 20 minutes
or until tender.

Drain and mash.

Combine with remaining ingredients and stir until smooth.

Spoon mixture into lightly greased 11 x 7 x 3 baking dish.

Bake in oven for 1 hour or until firm.

Candied Yams

serves 8 to 10

5 large yams or sweet potatoes, peeled and chunked
3/4 cup sugar
1 stick unsalted butter, sliced
1 teaspoon freshly grated nutmeg
1 tablespoon vanilla extract
1 teaspoon lemon extract
2 tablespoons light brown sugar
1/2 cup water

Combine all ingredients and cook on low to medium heat for 20 to 30 minutes.

Remember that candied yams should be soft but not mushy.

Vegetable Extravaganza

serves 10 to 12

1 cup fresh peas, shelled
1 cup broccoli florets
1/4 cup white onion, chopped
1 cup carrots, peeled and diced
1/2 cauliflower, separated into florets
1/4 cup green beans or string beans, chopped into 1-inch pieces
2 cups American or sharp Cheddar cheese, freshly grated
1 (10 3/4 ounce) can cream of mushroom soup
1 cup croutons

Preheat oven to 325° F.

Blanch vegetables in boiling water, 4 to 6 minutes; drain thoroughly.

Pour into lightly greased 1 1/2-quart casserole and add all but a few tablespoons of cheese.

Gently fold in soup.

Bake for 35 minutes.

Top with croutons and remaining cheese; bake for 5 minutes or until cheese is lightly browned.

Serve warm.

Submitted by Wayne Jackson of Baltimore, Maryland.

Strawberry Nut Salad

serves 10 to 15

1 (3-ounce) package strawberry-flavored gelatin
1 (1/4-ounce)package unflavored gelatin
1 pint fresh or frozen strawberries, thawed
14 ounces crushed pineapple
2 medium ripe bananas, mashed
1 cup chopped black walnuts or pecan halves
1 pint sour cream
2 1/4 cups water
iceberg or Bibb lettuce

Add 2 cups boiling water to strawberry-flavored gelatin and stir
thoroughly to dissolve.

Add unflavored gelatin to 1/4 cup cold water, let stand one
minute, then add to strawberry-flavored gelatin mixture.

Add fruit and nuts and mix well.

Pour half of mixture into a dish or decorative mold and put in
the freezer for 30 minutes.

After congealed, spread sour cream over top.

Add remaining gelatin and fruit mixture and refrigerate until
congealed, about 4 hours.

Serve cold over a bed of lettuce.

Desserts

Hot Banana Pudding
serves 20

12-ounce box vanilla wafers
4 to 6 bananas
5 eggs, separated
14 ounces evaporated milk
2 1/4 cups sugar
1 tablespoon vanilla extract
1 tablespoon cornstarch

Preheat oven to 400° F.

Slice bananas in half lengthwise.

Place vanilla wafers and bananas in baking dish in three equal layers; set aside.

Combine yolks, milk, sugar (reserving 2 tablespoons for meringue), vanilla extract, and cornstarch. Cook on medium heat for 15 minutes, stirring constantly.

Pour over layers of vanilla wafers and banana; let cool.

With electric mixer on medium speed, beat egg whites until firm peaks form, about 5 to 10 minutes, gradually adding 2 tablespoons of sugar.

Gently spread over custard.

Place in oven and let meringue brown for 5 to 7 minutes.

Serve immediately.

Blackberry Cobbler

serves 12 to 16

You can use just about any fruit in this cobbler. Use a medley of berries, sour cherries, or your grandmama's canned peaches.

7 cups fresh or frozen blackberries
2 sticks unsalted butter or margarine
1 1/2 cups milk
2 cups all-purpose flour
1/2 cup sugar
1 teaspoon vanilla extract
juice of half a lemon, strained

Preheat oven to 350° F.
Melt butter or margarine in 13 x 9 x 2-inch glass baking dish.
Combine milk, flour, and sugar; mix thoroughly.
Pour milk and flour mixture over melted butter or margarine.
Add vanilla extract and small amount of lemon juice to blackberries. Pour blackberries into middle of milk and flour mixture; do not stir.
Bake for 45 minutes or until golden brown.

Buttermilk Oatmeal Cookies

makes 5 dozen

1 cup vegetable shortening
2 large eggs
1 1/2 cups firmly packed light brown sugar
1/2 cup buttermilk
1 3/4 cups all-purpose flour
1 teaspoon baking soda
1 teaspoon baking powder
1 teaspoon salt
1 teaspoon freshly ground cinnamon
1 teaspoon freshly grated nutmeg
3 cups quick-cooking oats
1 cup raisins
1/2 cup black walnuts, chopped

Preheat oven to 400° F.

Cream shortening, eggs, and sugar until light and fluffy. Stir in
buttermilk.

Sift together flour, baking soda, baking powder, salt, cinnamon,
and nutmeg. Stir into creamed mixture.

Stir in oats, raisins, and nuts.

Drop by rounded, greased teaspoon onto greased cookie sheet.

Bake for 8 minutes and remove to a wire rack to cool
thoroughly.

Peanut Butter Cookies

makes 3 dozen

1/2 cup unsalted butter or margarine
1/2 cup peanut butter (creamy or chunky)
1/2 cup firmly packed light brown sugar
1 large egg, beaten
1/2 tablespoon vanilla extract
1 1/4 cup sifted all-purpose flour
3/4 teaspoon baking soda
1/2 teaspoon salt
1/2 cup granulated sugar

Preheat oven to 375° F.

Cream butter or margarine, peanut butter, brown sugar, egg, and
vanilla extract until light and fluffy.

Sift together flour, baking soda, and salt; blend into creamed
mixture.

Shape into 1-inch balls and roll in granulated sugar.

Place balls 2 inches apart on an ungreased cookie sheet and flat-
ten with the tines of a fork in a crosshatch pattern.

Bake in batches on the middle rack of the oven for
10 to 12 minutes.

Allow to cool slightly on a wire rack before serving.

Mama Alice

My godmother Alice Jackson couldn't read or write, but she always tried to help everyone as best she could. Especially young girls who were having babies before they were ready. She tried to get them to stay in school, get their education, and think about that job. Mama Alice announced it and pronounced it.

To my knowledge she wasn't saved but she had a lot of love in her heart for all kinds of people. Every birthday—for me and I swan I don't know how many more—she would give a nice card and a couple of crisp, new bills. She was as generous to all of us as she was to her own sons, Barnett and Booderack, and that's why we all called her Mama Alice. I always wondered how a lady who did day work could have anything left over to honor birthdays. Maybe she did without, just because she knew children like to have a little something to honor them on their day.

When Mama Alice had a stroke and went to live her last in a nursing home, a lot of those she'd honored with birthday cards saw to it that she wasn't lonely, had her fresh nightgowns, and whatever she needed. She passed quietly in her seventies surrounded by all those grown-up birthday babies.

Every time I went down to Georgia from Baltimore in the summertime, Mama Alice would take my request for this pie. Think of her when you make Mama Alice's lemon pie.

Mama Alice's Old-Fashioned Lemon Pie

makes 1 9-inch pie

CRUST

8 ounces of
graham cracker
crumbs
2 tablespoons sugar
small amount of
water
1/2 stick of
unsalted butter

FILLING

4 egg yolks
7 ounces
sweetened
condensed milk
1/2 cup freshly
squeezed lemon
juice, strained

MERINGUE

4 egg whites
1/4 teaspoon cream
of tartar

TO MAKE THE CRUST

Preheat oven to 325° F.

Combine crumbs and sugar in a medium mixing bowl, sprinkle with water and mix. Pat crumbs into a 9-inch pie pan and brush with melted butter.

Bake in oven for 5 to 10 minutes, or until slightly brown. Cool 10 to 15 minutes.

TO MAKE THE FILLING

Combine egg yolks and condensed milk in medium mixing bowl. With electric mixer, beat on medium speed for 5 minutes. Add lemon juice to egg yolk mixture and beat an additional 5 minutes. Pour mixture into crust.

TO MAKE THE MERINGUE

Preheat oven to 400° F. Combine egg whites and cream of tartar in copper, glass, or plastic bowl. With electric mixer, beat on high speed for 5 to 10 minutes until stiff peaks form. Gently spread egg whites over lemon filling.

Bake 5 to 7 minutes until meringue is golden brown. Let stand at room temperature for 3 hours before serving.

The Impossible Pie

makes 1 10-inch pie

I call it The Impossible Pie because its impossible to mess up and impossible not to love.

4 eggs
1/2 stick margarine, melted
1 cup sweetened coconut flakes
1/2 cup baking mix
1/2 tablespoon vanilla extract
1/2 cup sugar

Preheat oven to 350° F.
Place all ingredients in a blender.
Blend on low speed for 30 seconds.
Pour contents into an ungreased 10-inch pie tin.
Bake for 50 minutes.

Desserts

Homemade Ice Cream

serves 15 to 20

8 eggs
2 to 3 cups sugar
1 to 2 tablespoons vanilla extract
3 to 5 cups fruit of choice (strawberries, peaches, etc.), quartered
2 pints whipping cream
whole milk
crushed ice
rock salt

Combine eggs, sugar, vanilla extract, and 1 cup fruit. Beat until blended and let set for 15 minutes to allow sugar to dissolve. Pour into freezer can. Add whipping cream and remaining fruit.
Before churning, add alternating layers of crushed ice and rock salt to freezer bucket until full. Fill to freeze line with milk and begin to churn.

Bo Weaver's
Delicious Pound Cake
makes 1 cake

**Butter and eggs must be at room temperature to make this hefty cake
its best. This recipe is for the old-fashioned pound cake—a pound of this,
that, and the other. It freezes well too.**

4 sticks unsalted butter, softened
10 medium eggs
3 cups sugar
3 cups all-purpose flour, sifted
2 teaspoons lemon or vanilla extract
confectioners sugar

Preheat oven to 325° F. Butter and flour a 9 x 3-inch round cake
pan. Using an electric mixer cream the butter until fluffy. Add
the sugar gradually, beating until fluffy. Add eggs one at a
time, beating well after each addition. Gradually add flour
mixture. Add lemon or vanilla extract and mix thoroughly.
Pour mixture into pan. Bake in 325° oven for 1 hour and
15 minutes, or until cake tester comes out clean.
Cool 10 minutes before removing from pan, then cool thoroughly on a wire rack. Dust with 4x confectioners' sugar
before serving.

**Put a paper doily on the cake before dusting with confectioners sugar.
Carefully remove to reveal a decorative design.**

Desserts

Cold-Oven Pound Cake

makes 1 cake

This cake is so good you'll want to make one for yourself and one for your nice neighbor across the street.

1/2 stick unsalted butter or margarine
1 pound confectioners sugar
4 eggs
1 cup warm water
3 cups all-purpose flour
2 teaspoons vanilla extract
1 teaspoon baking powder
1/2 to 1 cup black walnuts, coarsely chopped

Butter and flour a 9 x 3-inch round cake pan.

Sift together flour and baking powder. Using an electric mixer, cream the butter until fluffy. Add the confectioners sugar gradually, beating until fluffy. Add eggs one at a time, beating well after each addition. Add water and vanilla extract. Gradually add flour mixture and mix thoroughly. Fold in walnuts.

Pour mixture into pan.

Put in a cold oven and turn temperature to 350° F. Bake for 50 to 60 minutes, or until cake tester comes out clean.

Submitted by Ms. Lenora Elton MacKenzie (Me Mae) of Baltimore, Maryland.

Punch Bowl Cake

serves 25 to 30

1/2 pound cake
10 ripe bananas, sliced in coins
2 quarts fresh strawberries, sliced
2 (10-ounce) cans crushed pineapple, well drained
2 cups chopped pecans
8 ounces whipped topping
1 (6-ounce) jar maraschino cherries, well drained
2 (3-ounce) packages strawberry-flavored gelatin

Cover bottom of punch bowl with thin slices of pound cake.

Cover pound cake with layer of bananas, strawberries, pineapple, and pecans.

Spread layer of whipped topping over fruit and nut layer.

Repeat layering until ingredients are gone.

Prepare gelatin according to directions on box; pour over dessert.

Put final layer of whipped topping on top and garnish with cherries.

Refrigerate until gelatin sets, about 4 hours.

Keep refrigerated until ready to serve.